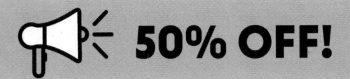

Free DVD **FREE** Free DVD

Essential Test Tips Video from Trivium Test Prep

Dear Customer,

Thank you for purchasing from Trivium Test Prep! Whether you're looking to join the military, get into college, or advance your career, we're honored to be a part of your journey.

To show our appreciation (and to help you relieve a little of that test-prep stress), we're offering a **FREE *Praxis Essential Test Tips* Video** by Trivium Test Prep. Our video includes 35 test preparation strategies that will help keep you calm and collected before and during your big exam. All we ask is that you email us your feedback and describe your experience with our product. Amazing, awful, or just so-so: we want to hear what you have to say!

To receive your **FREE *Praxis Essential Test Tips* Video**, please email us at 5star@ triviumtestprep.com. Include "Free 5 Star" in the subject line and the following information in your email:

1. The title of the product you purchased.

2. Your rating from 1 – 5 (with 5 being the best).

3. Your feedback about the product, including how our materials helped you meet your goals and ways in which we can improve our products.

4. Your full name and shipping address so we can send your **FREE *Praxis Essential Test Tips* Video**.

If you have any questions or concerns please feel free to contact us directly at 5star@triviumtestprep.com.

Thank you, and good luck with your studies!

Praxis Teaching Reading Elementary 5205 Study Guide

2 Practice Test and Exam Prep for
the Praxis 5205 [3rd Edition]

Eric Canizales

TABLE OF CONTENTS

ONLINE RESOURCES

T rivium includes online resources with the purchase of this study guide to help you fully prepare for the exam.

From Stress to Success

Watch "From Stress to Success," a brief but insightful YouTube video that offers the tips, tricks, and secrets experts use to score higher on the exam.

Flashcards

Trivium's flash cards allow you to review important terms easily on your computer or smartphone.

Cheat Sheets

Review the core skills you need to master the exam with easy-to-read Cheat Sheets.

Feedback

Leave a review, send us helpful feedback, or sign up for Cirrus promotions—including free books!

Access these materials at: www.cirrustestprep.com/praxis-reading-5205-online-resources

Introduction

Congratulations on choosing to take the Praxis Teaching Reading: Elementary (5205) exam! By purchasing this book, you've taken the first step toward becoming an elementary reading specialist.

This guide will provide you with a detailed overview of the Praxis Teaching Reading: Elementary (5205) exam, so you know exactly what to expect on test day. We'll take you through all the concepts covered on the exam and give you the opportunity to test your knowledge with practice questions. Even if it's been a while since you last took a major test, don't worry; we'll make sure you're more than ready!

What is the Praxis?

Praxis Series tests are a part of teaching licensure in approximately forty states. Each state uses the tests and scores in different ways, so be sure to check the certification requirements in your state by visiting www.ets.org/praxis/states. There, you will find information detailing the role of Praxis tests in determining teaching certification in your state, what scores are required, and how to transfer Praxis scores from one state to another.

What's on the Praxis Teaching Reading: Elementary (5205) Exam?

You will have two hours to answer ninety-three questions. Ninety questions are multiple choice; three are constructed response. These questions will cover a range of topics that test your understanding of the five core aspects of reading instruction: phonemic awareness, phonics, fluency, comprehension, and vocabulary.

You will be responding to situations involving individual students in grades ranging from kindergarten through high school—including students with disabilities—as well as situations involving classes as a whole.

What's on the Praxis Teaching Reading: Elementary (5205) Exam?		
Subject	**Approximate Number of Questions**	**Percentage per Subject**
Phonological and Phonemic Awareness including Emergent Literacy	14 multiple-choice questions	11%
Phonics and Decoding	18 multiple-choice questions	15%
Vocabulary and Fluency	21 multiple-choice questions	18%
Comprehension of Literary and Informational Text	21 multiple-choice questions	18%
Writing	16 multiple-choice questions	13%

What's on the Praxis Teaching Reading: Elementary (5205) Exam?		
Subject	Approximate Number of Questions	Percentage per Subject
Assessment and Instructional Decision-Making	3 constructed- response questions	25%
Total	90 multiple choice; 3 constructed response	2 hours 30 minutes

Phonological and Phonemic Awareness and Emergent Literacy questions cover aspects of expressive and receptive language skills, concepts of print, phonemic and phonological awareness, their relationship, and the development of encoding and decoding skills. Understand the progression of various skills (e.g., rhyme response, onset and rime manipulation, word and syllable awareness) and at what age these should be learned. You should also know the instructional and assessment techniques relevant to these skills.

Phonics and Decoding questions test your understanding of phonics patters and rules, ensuring your knowledge of simple and complex systematic and recursive phonics instruction. You should know the types of syllables, syllabication principles, and how to identify phonetically regular and irregular words as well as various strategies for delivering and modifying phonics instruction and helping students develop word solving strategies.

Vocabulary and Fluency questions require knowledge of factors that affect word meaning, such as context, word relationships, prefixes, suffixes, and grammatical functions. You should know the direct and indirect methods of vocabulary instruction, how to choose appropriate vocabulary words, and ways to evaluate growth in vocabulary knowledge. Expect to also be tested on elements of reading fluency and instructional strategies to improve fluency as well as the relationship between fluency and comprehension.

For Comprehension of Literary and Informational Text questions, review factors that affect comprehension: vocabulary, cultural and linguistic backgrounds, language structures, features of text, and so forth. Expect to be tested on instructional strategies for developing and assessing comprehension skills and understand Scarborough's strands of the Reading Rope and the four phases of word reading and reading development per Ehri.

Writing questions test your knowledge of theoretical frameworks such as the Simple View and Not So Simple View of Writing as well as systematic, explicit methods for teaching writing, spelling and grammar, and integrating writing with reading instruction. Prepare for questions on using multisensory teaching approaches to teach the structure of written language and how to use technology in the writing process.

The Assessment and Instructional Decision-Making section contains constructed-response questions about teaching and assessment practices. These test your ability to successfully encourage student participation, differentiate instruction, and use assessment data to inform instruction. You will also be tested on applying informal and formal methods of summative assessment and progress monitoring as well as making modifications or accommodations for diverse learners.

How is the Praxis Teaching Reading (5204) Exam Scored?

Each multiple-choice question on the Praxis Teaching Reading: Elementary (5205) exam is worth one raw point, and your raw score is the total number of questions answered correctly. The constructed-response questions are scored by two or more professional educators; these results are added to your raw score. The raw score will be converted to a scaled score specific to the Teaching Reading exam.

The exam will include pretest questions that do not count towards your score. Since there is no penalty for wrong answers, you should answer every question on the test.

How is the Praxis Teaching Reading: Elementary (5205) Exam Administered?

The exam is administered in a computerized format internationally, at universities, and at Prometric testing centers across the nation. Visit https://www.ets.org/praxis to find a convenient location and check requirements before registering to take the Praxis exam. Be sure to bring proper identification on the day of the test. You will have the opportunity to review how to answer questions and navigate the test before the exam begins.

Your score report will be accessible on your online Praxis account on the score report date corresponding to your testing window. This report will include your raw and scaled scores, the range of possible scores, the total raw points available in each category, and whether you passed or failed the exam. (Passing scores vary by state.)

About Cirrus Test Prep

Cirrus Test Prep study guides are designed by current and former educators and are tailored to meet your needs as an incoming educator. Our guides offer all the resources necessary to help you pass teacher certification exams across the nation.

Cirrus clouds are graceful, wispy clouds characterized by their high altitude. Just like cirrus clouds, Cirrus Test Prep's goal is to help educators "aim high" when it comes to obtaining their teacher certification and entering the classroom.

About This Guide

This guide will help you master the most important test topics and develop critical test-taking skills. We have built features into our books to prepare you for your exam and increase your score. Along with a detailed summary of the test's format, content, and scoring, we offer an in-depth overview of the content knowledge required to pass the exam. Our sidebars provide interesting information, highlight key ideas, and review content so that you can solidify your understanding of the exam's concepts. Test your knowledge with sample questions and detailed answer explanations in the text that help you think through the problems on the exam and practice questions that reflect the content and format of the Praxis Teaching Rading: Elementary exam. We're pleased you've chosen Cirrus to be a part of your professional journey!

1. Emergent Literacy

Oral Language Skills

Before students learn to read, they learn to speak and listen. This process relies on both **receptive language**, the ability to understand what is being said, and **expressive language**, the ability to use language to communicate ideas appropriately.

Techniques for developing oral language skills in children include:

▶ asking students to describe objects in the room or that they see out the window or outside on a nature walk

▶ asking students to describe how two objects or pictures are similar or different

▶ encouraging play with props in the dramatic play center

▶ encouraging students to pretend to be a character from a story

▶ asking students to describe another person or themselves aloud

- ➢ Giving students oral directions to follow
- ➢ Asking students to restate what they have heard

Sample Question

1) A kindergarten teacher wants to develop receptive language skills in students. Which activity best meets this goal?
   A. Students introduce themselves to each other and tell about their family.
   B. Students sing along with a song they have memorized.
   C. Students listen to a story and think about which character they liked best.
   D. Students follow oral directions to locate a specific place on the playground.

Print Awareness and Letter Recognition

Print awareness involves a basic understanding of the nature of reading: we read from left to right and top to bottom, and we are reading words on a page. Very young children without solid print awareness may believe that meaning is gleaned from pictures on a page rather than words. Some younger children may understand that books convey meaning but may not quite know how. Teachers may see these children modeling reading a book upside down.

Concepts of print are the principles that must be mastered before learning to read and are key to print awareness. These principles include knowledge and identification of a word, letter, and sentence; knowledge of the many uses of print; and knowledge of the overarching structure of a book or story (title, beginning, middle, end).

Many young students have some print awareness through environmental print. **Environmental print** describes the words children see regularly in their environment, like product names, street signs, business names, and menus at restaurants. Teachers can use popular environmental print, like the

names and logos of popular children's products, stores, and restaurants, to encourage pre-readers to "read" these words.

Teachers should also consider using environmental print in each of their students' home languages in the classroom. For example, a teacher might label the door in English, Spanish, Thai, and Vietnamese. This builds confidence and familiarity and reinforces the idea that these words in languages other than English also have meaning.

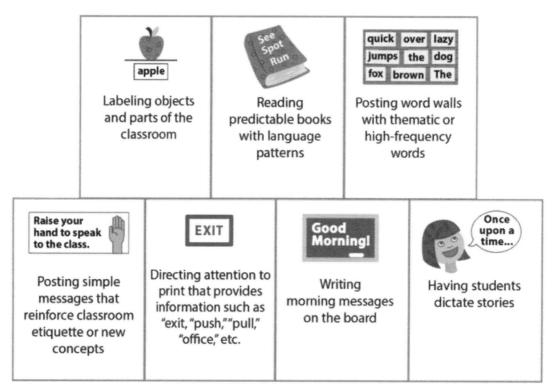

Figure 1.1. Concepts of Print Classroom Strategies

Teaching concepts of print should include showing students that print is read from left to right and top to bottom and that the reader's eyes move from the end of one line to the start of the next line in what is known as a **return sweep**. Students should also learn the parts of a book such as the cover, title, and illustrations.

Teachers should have young students point to words on a page and also point to words (rather than pictures) themselves during storybook reading. This will reinforce concepts of print and help students develop print awareness. Such practice will help even very young students begin to understand that while both the pictures and words on the page contribute to the overall meaning, the part being read is the words, not the pictures.

Assessing print awareness can be done informally and would most likely involve use of a book. Then, the student can be asked to:

➢ Point to the book cover, title, author, and illustration.

➢ Move their hand or finger to identify the direction the text is read.

➢ Point to a sentence, word, and letter.

Another early emergent literacy skill is identifying letters, both upper and lower case. Young students should be introduced to letters in various fonts, such as script and print. Strategies for helping students identify letters include:

➢ Having students trace letters as they say their names

➢ Asking students to identify letters in environmental print

➢ Having students play with and talk about tactile representations of letters

➢ Playing games or sorts with letters (such as upper case vs. lower case or print vs. script)

➢ Teaching and singing the alphabet song (though this only reinforces the names of the letters, not their identification)

Sample Question

2) Which activity will help gauge a student's print awareness?
   A. asking him to recount story events
   B. asking him to point to a sentence
   C. asking him to write the letter p
   D. asking him what sound p makes

Phonological Awareness

Phonological awareness is the general ability to understand that within the structure of oral language, there are subparts. These parts include individual words; **syllables**, or units (typically containing a single vowel sound) within words; **onsets**, or the beginning consonant sounds of words (*sw*-im); and **rimes**, or the letters which follow (sw-*im*).

Having phonological awareness is a crucial early stage in learning to read and write, and it can be fostered in the initial levels through singing songs and repeating rhyming words and phrases. **Alliteration**, or the repetition of beginning sounds, is another way to build phonological awareness. Nursery rhymes like "Peter Piper Picked a Peck of Pickled Peppers" often use alliteration to help students develop phonological awareness.

> **Helpful Hint**
>
> Remember that onsets are the first part of the word, or the first "button" readers see—the ON button. Rimes are the parts of the word that rhyme such as c-*at*, h-*at*, b-*at*, and so on.

Any activities or speech that seeks to break language into component parts or that help establish an understanding of syllables, onsets, and rimes—"Would *Son*-ya come to circle time?" "Do you want a *c*-at or a *h*-at for your birthday?"—are good choices for helping students begin to recognize the parts within language.

Producing and creating oral rhymes	Singing songs with alliteration	Clapping and other hand movements (e.g., clapping for onsets and rimes in words, clapping for each word in a sentence)	Learning alphabet songs
Listening for and identifying the sounds at the beginning, middle, and end of CVC words	Orally blending, segmenting, and manipulating phonemes in words	Sorting pictures according to beginning or ending sound	Using finger spelling, which is a form of sign language that uses the hands to represent letters

Figure 1.2. Phonological Awareness Classroom Strategies Sample Question

3) A teacher has a group of picture cards that has various objects and animals on them. She holds up a picture of a dog. What question should the teacher ask students to help their development of phonological awareness?

A. What word rhymes with *dog*?
B. How many letters are in the word *dog*?
C. Does *dog* have a long or short vowel sound?
D. How do we write *dog* with an uppercase d?

Phonemes

Phonemes are distinct units of sound and are the basic units of language. There are twenty-six letters in the alphabet, and most researchers agree that there are at least forty-four phonemes in English. Some letters represent different phonemes, and some phonemes are made up of more than one letter. There are eighteen consonant phonemes, such as /r/ and /t/, and fifteen vowel phonemes, such as /Ā/ and /oi/. There are six *r*-controlled vowels, such as /Ä/, and five digraphs, such as /ch/ and /sh/. **Phonetics** is the study and classification of phonemes or sounds and is part of explicit, systematic phonics instruction.

Phoneme	Example	Phoneme	Example	Phoneme	Example
Consonants		**Vowels**		**R-Controlled Vowels**	
/b/	bat	/a/	lap	/ã/	hair
/d/	dog	/ā/	late	/ä/	art
/f/	fish	/e/	bet	/û/	dirt
/g/	goat	/ē/	see	/ô/	draw
/h/	hat	/i/	hit	/ēə/	rear
/j/	jump	/ī/	ride	/üə/	sure
/k/	kick	/o/	hop	**Digraphs**	
/l/	laugh	/ō/	rope	/zh/	measure
/m/	milk	/oo/	look	/ch/	chick
/n/	no	/u/	cut	/sh/	shout
/p/	pot	/ū/	cute	/th/	think
/r/	rat	/y/ or /ü/	you	/ng/	bring
/s/	sit	/oi/	oil		
/t/	toss	/ow/	how		
/v/	vote	/ə/ (schwa)	syringe		
/w/	walk				
/y/	yak				
/z/	zoo				

Phonemic awareness refers to the knowledge of and ability to use phonemes. Phonemic awareness is similar to phonological awareness. However, phonological awareness refers to parts of words (like onset and rime and syllables) and parts of sentences. Phonemic awareness is more about individual sounds in words or phonemes. Phonological awareness is a precursor to phonemic awareness.

Because phonemic awareness does not come naturally, students need explicit instruction to master it. It is often best to work with students in small groups because proficiency levels of phonemic awareness may vary substantially.

Phoneme blending involves putting sounds together to make words. To work on phoneme blending, teachers can say sounds and ask students what word is made: "I like /ch/ /ee/ /z/. What do I like? That's right, I like cheese." Teachers can also ask students to repeat the sounds in words during circle time or storybook reading: "The car went vvvvv-rrrrr-oooo-m!"

Phoneme segmentation is the inverse of phoneme blending and involves sounding out a word. The use of **Elkonin boxes**, or the placement of tiles or letters that correspond with each phoneme, is a helpful activity for phoneme segmentation.

Figure 1.3. Elkonin Box

Phoneme segmentation is important both for reading and spelling a word. More advanced phonemic awareness activities include **phoneme deletion**, in which a phoneme is removed to make a new word (e.g., ramp – /p/ = ram) and **phoneme substitution**, in which one phoneme is changed to make a new word (e.g., fla/t/ to fla/p/).

Early childhood teachers should work on phonemic awareness with students in a variety of contexts. For example, teachers can ask students questions like "What word could I make if I took away the first letter of *cow*?" Alphabet boards, letter cards, and alphabet sorters provide fun and effective practice for phonemic awareness.

Educators should remember that students will have varying backgrounds, skill levels, English language proficiencies, and possibly speech and language delays and hearing loss. When planning inclusive activities, teachers may need to modify activities for some students. Also, phonemes are not the same in

all languages. Students from non-English-speaking households will need additional practice in English phonemes.

Phonemic awareness activities usually occur in a sequence from simplest to most difficult.

1.   Students usually understand the concepts of rhyme and alliteration first, generally in preschool or around age 3-4. These skills can be practiced by listening to and singing rhyming and alliterative songs and stories. Rhyme is often taught explicitly as well: students think of words that rhyme, or they listen to and repeat favorite nursery rhymes or stories.

2.   The recognition of syllables in words is usually the next step, which usually happens in pre-kindergarten or age 4-5. Students can clap out syllables in multisyllable words or stomp feet while saying each syllable.

3.   Identification of **onsets**, or the first sound of a word (*cat*), and **rime**, or the remaining letters of the word (*cat*) is next. Most students will have this skill in kindergarten or by age 6. Scrambled onset/rime word cards or word families (*tug, bug, lug, rug*) are two of the many strategies for developing recognition of these concepts.

4.   Once students are familiar with onset and rime, they can usually "hear" and understand individual letter sounds within words, also typically by age 6. Students should have plenty of practice with the more basic concepts and easier skills before practicing blending (adding sounds together) or segmenting (pulling sounds apart).

5. Phoneme blending, segmentation, and manipulation are more advanced skills that may take longer for some students. However, by age 6-7 or first grade, most students will be able to participate in these types of exercises.

6. Phoneme deletion is often hardest for students to master, especially if the sound involves a blend. However, by age 8-9, most students should be able to delete sounds, even within blends. For example, they should be able to say "Stand" without the "/t/."

Sample Question

4) Mark, a kindergartner, has mastered his letter sounds. He is sitting at the oral reading table with Ms. Hayes, trying to read a short sentence. He gets stuck on the word *glad* and stops reading. Which strategy might Ms. Hayes have Mark use?
   A. phoneme substitution
   B. phoneme blending
   C. phoneme segmentation
   D. thinking of a rhyming word

ANSWER KEY

1) **D.** This is receptive language because it involves students listening and understanding what is being said.

2) **B.** Knowing the difference between a letter, a word, and a sentence is an important component of print awareness.

3) **A.** Rhyming activities help students develop phonological awareness.

4) **C.** Phoneme segmentation is the strategy of "sounding out." Mark could be encouraged to sound out both phonemes "gl-ad."

2. Beginning Literacy

Phonics

Phonics is an age-old strategy for helping students read by connecting written language to spoken language or by correlating certain sounds with certain letters or groups of letters. Whereas phonological and phonemic awareness are more concerned with sounds, phonics focuses on the relationship between sounds and letters or letter patterns.

Phonics is a **recursive** process because it involves the repeated application of certain procedures or rules to decode text. Effective phonics is also **systematic** because it follows a logical sequence where students progress and build upon previously mastered knowledge. Phonics instruction should also be **explicit** or taught via direct instruction as opposed to implicit means.

Essential to phonics instruction is a subset of the alphabetic principle—**letter-sound correspondence** also known as **phoneme-grapheme correspondence**. This correspondence is simply the knowledge of a phoneme (sound) associated with a given letter. Letter-sound correspondence is a foundational skill for effective phonics instruction, as most phonics strategies require students to draw from this memory bank of letter sounds.

Alphabetic Principle

The **alphabetic principle** presumes an understanding that words are made up of written letters that represent spoken sounds. Students should be given many opportunities to develop letter-sound correspondence, or the recognition and association of a letter with its sound.

There is no firm rule on the pace at which the letter sounds should be mastered. Most experts agree that high-frequency letters should be introduced first, as well as those that allow children to sound out short words quickly. It is sometimes easier for children to master simple sounds like /t/ and /s/ before more challenging or confusing sounds like /b/, /d/, and /i/.

> #### Did You Know?
>
> Most strategies for introducing students to the letter sounds draw on **high-frequency letter-sound correspondence**, whereby the most frequent and useful letter sounds are taught first. This allows students to begin reading as soon as possible without having to wait for mastery of each letter sound.

Regardless of how teachers practice the alphabetic principle (e.g., a letter of the week or teaching the letters in succession), they should recognize that repetition is key. Students should have many opportunities to practice each letter and sound. Letter sounds should be taught explicitly and in isolation from one another first. Then students can practice saying the sounds of letters and sounding out simple words in context. Strategies for teaching the alphabetic principle and letter-sound correspondence include:

▶ Begin instruction with lowercase letters, as these are the primary letters used in forming words.

▶ Avoid overemphasis of letter *names* and focus primarily on letter *sounds*. Students do not need to know letter names to learn to read, and some may be confused by the distinction between the letter name and letter sound.

▶ Teach easy consonants first, followed by easy vowel sounds, introducing a new sound every two or three days.

▶ Teach the most common sound a letter makes first. For example, the letter *g* should be associated with the sound it makes in *grass* before associating it with the sound it makes in *rage*.

▶ Teach letters that look similar and/or have somewhat similar sounds (e.g., /b/ and /d/ or /m/ and /n/) separately and to limit confusion.

▶ Model the correct pronunciation when teaching letter sounds, introducing continuous sounds (*f, l, m, n, r, s, v, w, y,* and *z*) before stop sounds (*b, c, d, g, j, k, p, q, t*). Stop sounds require control to pronounce correctly (/b/ for *b* vs. "buh" for *b*).

▶ Teach short vowel sounds before long vowel sounds. This is practical and allows for young readers to begin to sound out short consonant-vowel-consonant (CVC) words like *dig* and *run*.

Some activities that promote letter-sound correspondence include:

▶ Using letter-sound charts or letter-sound flashcards with or without picture cues with individual students, small groups, or the entire class. The "I say, you say, we say" method can be used effectively with these tools.

▶ Creating alphabet boards or even a computer keyboard with lowercase letters taped over the appropriate keys for instructional or assessment activities. As the teacher says a sound, students can point to the letter, type it, or move a tile over it.

▶ Having students trace or form lowercase letters with pens or pencils or in sand or shaving cream while saying the sound the letter makes. This can develop fine motor skills and reinforce letter-sound correspondence.

▶ Having students sort items into groups or piles based on initial letter sound. For example, students could place all the toy animals or pictures of animals with a /c/ sound in one group or pile.

Did You Know?
The "alphabet song" was copyrighted in 1835 but is actually an adaptation of a Mozart melody.

▶ Using alphabet picture books for guided storybook reading, stopping to reinforce and practice letter sounds. *Chicka Chicka Boom Boom* by Bill Martin and John Archambault and *Eating the Alphabet* by Lois Ehlert are popular choices.

▶ Having students draw a line around, color in, or circle all items on the page that begin with a given letter sound.

Sample Question

1) Which activity is MOST appropriate for students to practice the alphabetic principle?
   A. having them sort toy animals into tubs based on the initial letter sound of the animal's name
   B. asking them to help clap out the syllables in a student's name
   C. asking them to point to a sentence on a page
   D. having them remove a sound from a word and say the new word

Decoding

Phonics instruction draws on the strategy of **decoding**, or the ability to pronounce the sounds of written words orally and understand their meaning. Because of its focus on the specific sound structures of words, phonics instruction tends to involve more explicit, direct instruction. Some critics, however, believe it overemphasizes the mechanics of reading while sacrificing the enjoyment. Most classrooms today use an approach that balances inquiry-based student learning. This allows for the open exploration of high-interest literacy games and activities, with more direct instruction when necessary.

There are a number of structures for teaching decoding, such as a teacher-directed table or a mandatory computer-based phonics drill segment. But whatever the curriculum, it is highly likely that it will contain some phonics component. This approach is proven to work for most students and is adaptable to a variety of student skill levels and special learning needs. Further, explicit, systematic phonics instruction has been proven to be one of the most effective intervention strategies for students at risk of not meeting reading fluency goals.

Many words are **decodable**, meaning they follow basic principles of phonics. Students should be able to sound these words out once they master basic structural deviations, like long vowel sounds with a word ending in –*e*, and various digraphs, where two letters make a single sound such as /th/ and /ay/.

Other words are **non-decodable**, meaning they deviate from the standard rules of phonics. Typically, these words must simply be memorized through frequent exposure.

These words should be presented to students frequently so they can simply be memorized. These words must become **sight words**, or words that require no decoding because they are instantly recognized and read automatically. Some high-frequency decodable words, such as *get*, *and*, and *as* should also be memorized by sight to increase reading rate and fluency.

There are many lists of sight words. The most popular is the **Dolch Word List**, which contains 315 words determined to be the most frequently used in English. Early childhood teachers might post some of these high-frequency words around the classroom or encourage students to play games with sight word flashcards. Repetition will lead to mastery of these words and will help students read more quickly, fluently, and easily. Many state and national standards require students to recognize and read from a "research-based list." Some states and districts provide such lists to parents and students for practice at home.

> ### Did You Know?
>
> Fifty percent of all written material is made up of only one hundred of the most used words.

The balance between phonics and sight words is important. Students whose only reading strategy is sounding out may continue this even when they come across a word they know. This prevents automaticity and slows reading rate and, subsequently, comprehension. As students become more proficient readers, they should be encouraged to say words they know by sight or memory automatically without having to sound them out.

Educators should provide plenty of opportunities for students to be exposed to and read high-frequency words. Students can practice targeted activities aimed at memorization (such as paired drills or group activities) and read a variety of texts with these words. When students get stuck on high-frequency sight words, teachers can practice the "I say, you say, we say" method for immediate reinforcement.

Additionally, recognition of non-decodable words can be aided by a **multisensory approach**, or one that involves more than one sense. Visual, auditory, kinesthetic, and tactile activities can all be part of

helping students recognize these words. For example, students might place sight word tiles or strips in place as they say the words.

Sample Question

2) Sight words are unlike other words that early readers encounter because they
   A. lack typical structures that allow for sounding out.
   B. appear infrequently and only in certain genres.
   C. have multiple meanings based on context.
   D. should be memorized and recognized instantly.

3) Which word is MOST likely a non-decodable word?
   A. atlas
   B. flute
   C. sign
   D. save

4) At some point in their academic career, students will need to deviate from the exclusive use of a phonics through spelling model because
   A. not all words are spelled phonetically.
   B. it is only applicable to single-syllable words.
   C. the method does not address reading skills.
   D. it requires students to work in collaborative groups.

Best Practices for Teaching Phonics

Research indicates that a synthetic phonics approach is the most universal method of phonics instruction that can meet the needs of the most learners.

Synthetic phonics is one of the most common and effective types of phonics instruction. Students are explicitly taught to break down words into their component phonemes and sound them out. For example, a student would sound out the word *sheep* based on its three distinct phonemes, /sh/ /ee/ /p/. Synthetic phonics at its most basic level is associated with students "sounding out" unknown words as part of the decoding or meaning-making process. As students do this, they synthesize the sounds in the words to make meaning, hence the term *synthetic*.

Synthetic phonics discourages the practice of guessing at words based on initial letter sound (a common habit among many early readers) or other context or picture cues. It also teaches spelling and reading in tandem, with students sounding out or segmenting words before spelling them.

Synthetic phonics provides an explicit framework for decoding and allows students to tackle most words reliably. However, it is not without disadvantages. Some students rely on the strategy of sounding out far too long, and this can slow down reading rate and fluency and thus overall comprehension.

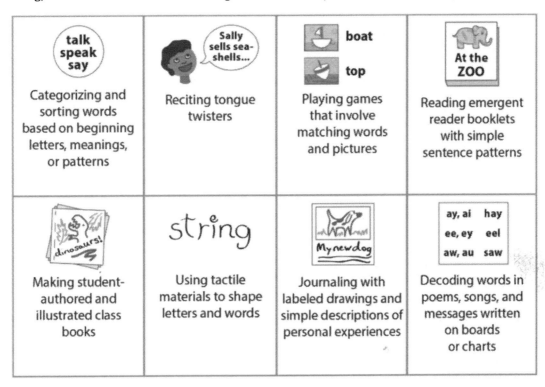

Figure 2.1. Phonics Classroom Strategies

Research also indicates that **systematic phonics instruction** that occurs in a particularly designed sequence is most effective. Typical approaches to explicit, systematic synthetic phonics instruction involve:

▶ teaching individual letter sounds

▶ teaching consonant blends

▶ teaching consonant digraphs

▶ teaching irregular/challenging vowel sounds like *r*-controlled vowels

When learning more advanced phonics structures, like blends and digraphs, students will need explicit instruction, as these are multiple letters that make a single sound. This is done through a combination of modeling and then guided and independent practice. At the early childhood levels (typically preschool to grade two or three), educators use small-group instruction to work with students more closely and provide more targeted oral feedback.

Did You Know?

Research draws a correlation between a teacher's knowledge of phonics and their effectiveness in teaching it.

Research also shows that phonics instruction is most effective when it also includes **connected texts**, or words in sentences and paragraphs instead of only in isolation or lists. These texts can be chosen for

practice and reinforcement with a particular skill or phonics structure and can allow students to practice new skills in an authentic context.

Practicing phonics skills in connected texts is different from an embedded phonics approach. In embedded phonics, phonics is only taught explicitly when understanding of connected texts breaks down. In a systematic, explicit phonics approach, phonetic structures are first introduced in isolation through direct instruction and practice. Only after this are connected texts introduced.

Phonics word patterns are introduced in sequence based on degree of difficulty:

1. VC or CVC words with simple (continuous) initial sounds (e.g., *man, pat, fin, at, on*)

2. VCC or CVCC words with initial continuous sounds (e.g., *ask, mash*)

3. CVC words with initial stop sounds (e.g., *cab, hit*)

4. CCVC words (easier blends with continuous sounds are generally taught before more challenging blends with stop sounds) (e.g., *flat, slap, stop, crab*)

5. CCVCC, CCCVC, or CCCVCC words with various levels of complexity are then introduced, including consonant digraphs (e.g., /sh/ /ch/) and vowel combinations (e.g., *ee, ea, oo*) as well as *r*-controlled vowels like *butter, wither, firm, germ* and so on.

While it is unlikely to find an entire text that contains only VC or CVC words or even only decodable words, shared/paired/choral reading strategies can help make texts accessible to all learners. Further, explicit practice with high-frequency sight words alongside phonics instruction is recommended. Instant recognition of common words will make decoding connected texts easier, faster, and more enjoyable for young readers. Above all, explicit and systematic phonics instruction should be calibrated for each student but should always aim at giving students the most useful and widely needed skills first. In this way, even young children can begin reading independently early, building confidence and possibly a life-long love of reading.

Phonics is also entwined with other literacy skills. Phonics helps student both in **encoding** or reading text and **decoding**, or forming text by spelling words.

Phonics through spelling is a combined approach whereby reading and spelling are taught in tandem. Students are taught to spell words phonetically by sounding them out or breaking them into their individual phonemes. The practice is based on the interconnectedness between the sounds of words and their spellings. This interconnectedness is what allows for **invented spelling**, whereby children learn to spell by first spelling all words phonetically. For example, they might spell *different* as *difrint*.

The advantage of this approach is that spelling is taught early and alongside reading. Many educators believe invented spelling is a natural part of the learning to write process.

Sample Questions

5) A kindergarten teacher is implementing a new synthetic phonics curriculum. The teacher observes a student working with the teaching assistant to read a short sentence: "He ran to the woods." The student becomes stuck on *woods*. Which question should the teaching assistant ask to stay aligned with synthetic phonics instruction?

    A. "What do the pictures tell you this word might be?"
    B. "What sound do the letters in the word make?"
    C. "Where would someone run?"
    D. "What other words do you know that rhyme with *wood*?"

6) Which word is the most difficult for students to decode and would thus be introduced toward the end of the phonics continuum?

    A. dirt
    B. stop
    C. call
    D. flat

Phonics Patterns for Beginning Readers

The **graphophonic cuing** system is based on applying sound (phoneme)-symbol (grapheme or letter) knowledge while reading. It is the most basic level of decoding and tends to be the least efficient since its focus is on individual units (e.g., letters and letter patterns) instead of larger chunks of text like words and ideas. However, it is the method by which students first learn to decode.

One common word-attack strategy based on graphophonics is knowledge of syllabication and syllable patterns. Students can be taught to break words into syllables and then identify the six **syllable patterns** to aid in decoding.

1. **Closed syllables** are the most common. They end in a consonant that causes the vowel to make a short sound. *Stretch*, *com*-puter, *bat*, and *backing* are all words with closed syllables and short vowel sounds.

2. **Open syllables** end in vowels and make long vowel sounds. *Ri*-val, *mi-cro*-phone, and *to*-tal are all examples of open syllables.

3. **Vowel-consonant-e syllables**, or VCE syllables, end in −*e*, which makes the final vowel sound long. De-*code*, *rude*, *bake* all have VCE syllables.

4. **Vowel teams** are two vowels next to each other that make a single sound. Some vowel teams are digraphs (only two letters), and others consist of three or four letters. *Laugh*, h*igh*, and h*ay* are examples of vowel teams.

5. **Consonant–le syllables**, or C–le syllables, are also sometimes called final syllables or final stable syllables. When these endings are joined with an open syllable, there is a long vowel sound and no double consonant. When they are joined with a closed syllable, there is a short vowel sound and double consonant. There are eleven −*le* patterns in English: −*ble* (*trouble*), −*gle* (*struggle*), −*zle* (*dazzle*), −*fle* (*trifle*), −*tle* (*battle*), −*dle* (*idle*), −*stle* (*whistle*), −*ckle* (*buckle*), −*ple* (*triple*), −*cle* (*recycle*), and −*kle* (*wrinkle*).

6. **R-controlled syllables**, also called vowel-*r* syllables, are often the most challenging. A vowel is followed by the letter *r*, which changes the way the vowel is pronounced. For example, in the word

water, the final syllable is not pronounced as a purely short *e* because it is an *r*-controlled vowel. Research suggests that explicit instruction and practice with *r*-controlled vowel forms (*er, ir, ur, ar, or*) and frequent repetition and review is essential to help students master these types of sounds to aid in decoding.

For graphophonic cuing to be most effective, readers must have some knowledge of the word they sound out to make meaning. For example, a first-grade student might be able to apply graphophonic cuing to successfully sound out the word *telepathy* and might figure out the correct pronunciation of this word while reading orally or even silently. However, this word is not truly decoded, or taken meaning from, unless the student can apply the graphophonic cues to existing knowledge of oral language vocabulary.

Other phonics patterns beyond syllable types are also essential for beginning phonics instruction. These include:

1. Consonant blends occur when two or more consonants work together to make a unique sound. Common consonant blends include: bl, cl, fl, cr, dr, tr, sp, st, tw, scr, and str, at the beginning of words and ct, ft, lt, nt, pt, st, and xt at the end of words. Students can learn consonant blends by working with **word families** or words that have a common pattern. For example, students can practice with words that begin with fl- such as fly, fling, flow, and flower.

2. Consonant digraphs occur when two consonants make a single sound. Common digraphs are sh, ph, th, wh, and ck.

3. Diphthongs are combinations of letters that make a combined vowel sound different from the standard a, e, i, o, u sounds. Examples of diphthongs are oi, ai, ea, igh, ey, ow, ough.

4. Schwa sounds are unstressed vowels that sound like a short /i/ or /u/. Examples of schwa sounds are a-gain (u-gain) and si-lent (sy-lint).

Teaching these more advanced phonics patterns can help students read more fluently, but should only introduced once students have mastered the basics such as letter sound correspondence and sounding out basic CVC words. Teaching these patterns usually involves use of word families as described. Students can practice reading and spelling grouped lists of words with common blends, digraphs, diphthongs, and schwa sounds. Word sorts, word bingo, and highlighted words or endings in connected texts with a certain phonics pattern are all good instructional activities to help students practice these concepts.

Sample Question

7) Which word contains both an open syllable and an *r*-controlled vowel?
   A. rigorous
   B. related
   C. hunger
   D. miser

Word Solving Strategies

The human brain uses three cuing systems to determine the meaning of words: semantic, syntactic, and grapho-phonetic (as described above). Together, these systems form word-analysis strategies or **word-**

solving strategies, sometimes referred to as word attack strategies, or methods of decoding unfamiliar words.

Semantic (Meaning) Cues

Semantic cues are cues to a word's meaning drawn from background knowledge or prior experience. Semantic cues are the brain's most efficient cuing system, since words are immediately retrieved from memory and processed. Semantic cues rely on students to activate knowledge and make reasonable predictions and inferences regarding a word's meaning. For example, in an informational text on fishing, the word *bobber* might come up. A reader familiar with fishing could activate this knowledge and recognize that "bobber" refers to a float used on a fishing line.

Semantic cuing is used in **cloze exercises**, in which words are removed from the text and students must supply them. To activate students' background knowledge to allow for maximum semantic cuing, some strategies include:

▶ Using metacognitive strategies and questions like "What type of word would make sense here?" "Does this meaning make sense in a text about _____?" "What qualities do _____ have that might lead to a clue of this word's meaning?"

▶ Having students make a list of words they predict might be used in the text after previewing its title, illustrations, and headings.

▶ Engaging students in scripted exercises in which they confirm predictions such as "The word _____ must mean _____ because I know that _____."

Semantic cues can also be based on the text itself. These are called **context clues** and do not necessarily have to be integrated with existing background knowledge. Context clues are any cues that help readers to determine word meaning in connected texts. They can be other words in the text or graphics. Students should be explicitly taught to identify other words in a sentence, paragraph, or passage that provide possible clues to the meaning of an unknown word. Students of all ages can also look to illustrations or charts to understand new words. This is particularly helpful with subject-specific vocabulary, such as terminology associated with organelles within plant cells.

Other words in the text are also essential in decoding **homographs** (words that are spelled the same but have different meanings) and **homonyms** (words that sound the same and may or may not be spelled the same but have different meanings). Educators often teach decoding homonyms and homographs explicitly. Teachers should direct students to the most commonly used homonyms to prepare them for encountering them in texts.

Context is usually the only way to determine the meaning of a homograph or multiple-meaning word. Homonyms can, at times, be decoded based on spelling alone, presuming the spelling differs, but this method should always be confirmed based on context to ensure correct decoding and understanding. Students can be asked to circle, underline, or highlight the other words in the text that "back up" their interpretations of multiple-meaning words.

Sample Question

8) Which activity would MOST likely help students develop the knowledge to use semantic cues effectively?
   A. reading books that provide information on a variety of places and cultures
   B. underlining confusing sentences and diagramming them
   C. reading a text aloud twice, once to oneself and once to a partner
   D. encouraging students to increase their reading rate to retain more information

Syntactic (Structural) Cues

Syntactic cues are based on the structure of language and are regarded as the brain's second-most efficient cuing system while reading. They include sentence structure and word order, structural clues within words, and structural analysis of the word.

A word's meaning can sometimes be clued or determined by its placement in a sentence. For example, figuring out whether a word is used as an adjective, noun, or verb can help with determining its meaning.

Structural clues within words such as **affixes** (prefixes and suffixes) and roots (base words with no affixes) can give clues to a word's meaning. This is sometimes referred to as **morphological analysis**, or the analysis of morphemes (the smallest units of meaning within words).

Students should be taught common Greek and Latin **roots** and their meanings as well as the meanings of common prefixes and suffixes. Students can practice roots and affixes by creating words with a single prefix like *geo* (e.g., *geography, geology, geopolitical, geoscience*) or with a single suffix like *–ly* (e.g., *friendly, happily, angrily*). Students can then determine what all the words they have created have in common. Students can also be given roots or base words and asked to create as many new words with affixes as possible. Students should then be encouraged to transfer this knowledge when they encounter new words in texts by using known roots or affixes as clues to the word's meaning.

Structural analysis of the word can also be a useful strategy. Students can decode compound words, for example, by breaking the word into its two component parts.

Sample Question

9) A student is stuck on the word *Istanbul* in the sentence "My father took a trip to Istanbul." She asks, "What is an Istanbul?" How best can the teacher encourage her to use syntactic cues to aid in determining the word's meaning?
   A. Have her break the word into its three syllables and sound out each syllable individually.
   B. Ask her if she has ever been to Turkey and, if so, what cities she visited.
   C. Cover up *Istanbul* and ask her what kind of word would most likely go in the blank.
   D. Ask her if she thinks the sentence "makes sense" as written or if the word "Istanbul" should be moved.

Vocabulary Development

An essential part of literacy is building and expanding vocabulary. The term **receptive vocabulary** refers to the words a student can read or hear and understand, and the term **expressive vocabulary** refers to the words a student can speak or write with correct use.

Vocabulary can and should also be broadened through a variety of strategies. Vocabulary knowledge makes reading more expedient and fluent, as readers can simply decode a word semantically without having to resort to other cuing systems. Vocabulary is developed through one of two ways. **Incidental vocabulary learning** occurs while reading, either independently or through teacher-guided oral reading activities. **Intentional vocabulary teaching** requires educators to more explicitly direct vocabulary acquisition. There are two methodologies to intentional vocabulary teaching: specific word instruction and word-learning strategies.

Teachers should match the method of vocabulary instruction with the word complexity. Typically, vocabulary is discussed in terms of tier. **Tier 1** are basic vocabulary words that are on or below grade level. These types of words typically do not require explicit instruction. **Tier 2** words are words that are essential for students' progress and are high frequency but may be more challenging words and may contain multiple meanings. These types of words will typically require direct instruction because they are essential for students to learn. Students will need more scaffolding and support with Tier 2 words. **Tier 3** words are also challenging but are domain-specific. Words like *magma, igneous,* and *tectonic* are all Tier 3 words related to science. These words generally also require some explicit instruction, though this may occur in the content-area classroom.

When selecting vocabulary words for instruction, the best course is teaching Tier 2 words via explicit instruction, especially Tier 2 words that are the most frequently used. However, when teaching a text that has several Tier 3 words, pre-teaching these words or giving students a list of these words and their definitions is a good practice.

Vocabulary instruction, like phonics instruction, should be recursive in offering opportunities for repeated practice and application, systematic in following a planned scope and sequence, and (at times) explicit, or involving direct instruction.

Specific Word Instruction

Specific word instruction involves activities that help learners acquire knowledge of new words.

Some strategies for specific word instruction are:

Predict-o-gram: Students are given a list of words. They then predict how these words will be used in a text. This strategy can be used effectively for both fiction and nonfiction texts, though it is most often used with fiction, as it can easily be integrated into existing knowledge about plot structure.

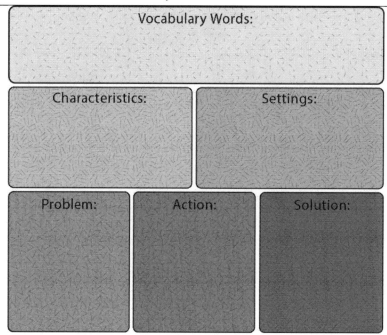

Figure 2.2. Predict-o-gram

Semantic impressions: Students are given a list of words in the order they appear in the text. The definition of each word is then briefly discussed by the teacher. Students write their own story using the words in the same order, using each word only once. They then read the text and compare their finished story to the original.

Semantic feature analysis, also called a semantic grid, is a graphic organizer that helps students think deeply about the features or properties of each vocabulary word.

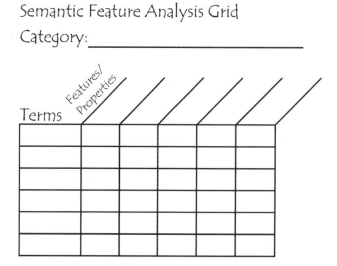

Figure 2.3. Semantic Feature Analysis

Semantic Gradients are continuums or lines that help students understand subtle shades of meaning among related words as well as broaden their overall vocabulary. Semantic gradients are usually formed

by putting two opposite words like miniscule and gigantic on a line and then filling in the middle with related (but not as strong) words.

miniscule   minute   tiny small average oversized large huge   gigantic

List-group-label is a semantic mapping strategy in which students brainstorm all the words they can think of that relate to a particular topic. They then divide the list of words into subcategories based on common features. For example, words like *dorsal fin*, *gills*, and *teeth* might be placed in the category of "parts of a fish's body."

Possible sentences: Students are given a list of vocabulary words from the text they will read. They then write a "possible" sentence for each word, illustrating the word's possible meaning. After reading the text, students return to their possible sentences to see if they were accurate or if the sentences need to be changed based on the word's actual meaning as revealed in the text.

OPIN (short for *Opinion*) is similar to a cloze exercise in which students fill in the blank with a word they think belongs in a sentence. Then, students break into groups to "defend" their word choice to other members of the group. This strategy helps reinforce other skills as students use context clues and background knowledge to justify their answers.

Sample Question

10) A teacher wants to incorporate creative writing into daily reading instruction. Which vocabulary-building activity is the MOST appropriate?
  A. list-group-label
  B. OPIN
  C. semantic impressions
  D. semantic grids

Word-Learning Strategies

In addition to specific word instruction, educators must use various strategies to help students learn new words they encounter in context. These strategies may be part of explicit lessons (e.g. a lesson on dictionary skills or morphology) or these may serve as a "toolkit" that students can use for independent vocabulary learning as they encounter new words while reading.

Using a dictionary, glossary, and thesaurus: In today's digital age, there are many opportunities for students to practice using resources to find the meaning of unfamiliar words. **Dictionary** skills are typically introduced around third grade and require explicit instruction on how to locate the word's pronunciation, etymology, parts of speech, and definition. Students should be taught to use both print and digital dictionaries. Many state standards require this knowledge, which is tested on annual accountability tests.

There are, of course, some limitations to dictionaries. They tend to focus only on a word's **denotation**, or literal meaning, when each word also has a **connotation**, or subtle or implied meaning. Readers must be taught to use **context clues** to determine connotation.

Thesauruses should also be used in reading and English classrooms. Students can learn when a thesaurus is the resource of choice and when a dictionary is more appropriate. Use of the **glossary**

should also be explicitly taught, and students should be encouraged to apply this skill across the content areas, as many of their texts for other courses will likely contain glossaries.

Morphemic or morphological analysis (see chapter 2) breaks apart the morphemes within words and analyzes them for meaning. Morphemic analysis should be taught explicitly as a unit of study and referred to frequently throughout reading instruction. Students should be asked to think about unfamiliar words in the context of their morphemes to help with decoding: "Are there roots or affixes I already know from other words?" "What does the word ending tell me?" "Is it a clue to the part of speech or singularity or plurality?"

Contextual analysis applies context clues to infer the meaning of unknown words. As mentioned above, contextual analysis can involve semantic or syntactic cues that aid in meaning. Some educators find strategies in annotating the text very helpful in teaching context clues. For example, students can put a question mark next to unknown words and then circle other words in the text that might provide clues to the word's meaning.

English language learners will need additional vocabulary-building practice, as vocabulary knowledge is one of the key foundations that leads to reading success for students with little background in English vocabulary. Specific strategies include picture dictionaries, teaching cognates, and teaching idioms, in addition to explicit and direct vocabulary instruction.

Sample Question

11) Which vocabulary term would MOST likely be included in a lesson on dictionary skills in a fourth-grade classroom?
  A. noun
  B. phonogram
  C. context
  D. origin

Fluency

Fluency refers to the rate, accuracy, and expression of a text when read. It is an important measure of a student's reading development because it affects comprehension and enjoyment of reading. Fluency is also related to vocabulary development because students cannot fluently read words they have no familiarity with.

Fluency has three components: rate, accuracy, and prosody. **Reading rate** is a measure of speed, generally calculated in words per minute. **Accuracy**, or the correct decoding of words, is entwined with rate when measuring fluency, since reading quickly but incorrectly is not desirable.

Did You Know?

All students will develop fluency at a different rate. Accurate assessments of fluency are developmentally appropriate and are NOT presented as high-stakes testing situations.

Fluency is not limited to oral reading, although it is virtually impossible to assess it during silent reading. Most educators rely on frequent oral reading assessments to determine student progress. (See chapter "Assessment and Instructional Decision-Making" for more discussion on how to assess reading fluency.)

Prosody, or the overall liveliness and expressiveness of reading, is another skill to nurture in students. Prosody includes appropriate pauses and changes in pitch and intonation based on punctuation and the overall

meaning of the piece. Teachers should model prosody as they read stories, passages, and even directions aloud. They should also give students plenty of opportunities for oral reading practice.

Fluent readers read with automaticity. **Automaticity** is the ability to easily recognize words automatically. Students who read with automaticity do not need to sound out or break down each word. They are able to read rapidly with little effort at the most basic levels of decoding. Automaticity only comes with automatic word recognition, which must be taught along with explicit phonics instruction aimed at decoding unfamiliar words.

Fluency is linked with comprehension because students who struggle to read and decode individual words will have difficulty comprehending entire sentences and paragraphs. Also, students who read at a slow rate may have trouble recalling what they have read. It is worth taking the time to listen to students read aloud as much as possible because sometimes students have developed certain strategies when reading silently and answering comprehension questions that may incorrectly suggest they are fluent readers. This will eventually catch up with students as the text complexity increases, so oral fluency should be monitored early and often.

Teachers must help students develop fluency at the phoneme, word, and passage level When students are developing fluency at the phoneme level, they are attempting to make and interpret the sounds in words. Teachers can support students through sound phonics instruction wherein such sounds are introduced and practiced sufficiently before students encounter them in connected texts. At the word level, teachers can remind students of these phonics structures (e.g. what sound does c and h make?). At the passage level, teachers can help students to adjust and monitor their comprehension and speed up or slow down their reading rate accordingly.

There are also many broad strategies for developing oral fluency in the classroom.

▶ **Timed repeated readings** are repeated readings of familiar texts at the independent reading level. Students read a text three or four times as the teacher records time and words correct per minute (WCPM).

▶ **Shared reading** occurs when teachers model oral fluency and students share the experience. They can do this by turning the pages and showing illustrations while asking students basic comprehension questions and to make predictions or inferences. Shared reading is also referred to as shared storybook reading, particularly in the early childhood setting.

▶ **Choral reading** involves the entire class or group reading a text aloud in unison. First, the teacher models the passage with appropriate rate and prosody. Students then read aloud, using their finger to follow the text. Choral reading helps develop confidence, prosody, and automaticity and can assist in sight word acquisition.

▶ In **paired reading** pairs of students take turns reading to each other. Often more fluent readers are paired with readers still developing fluency.

▶ **Reader's theater** uses drama or other texts with different roles or parts for students to read aloud with appropriate dramatic expression.

▶ **Audio-assisted reading** is a common strategy for students who lack fluency. Students follow along in a written text as they listen to a fluent reader read it aloud, usually on an audiobook.

▶ **Neurological impress** is a twist on choral reading whereby teacher and student read the same text at the same time while both following along with their fingers. This method is thought to "etch" the words in students' minds and help them develop automatic word recognition.

Sample Question

12) A second-grade teacher notices that his students often read in monotone during oral reading practice. Which strategy can the teacher use to help students develop prosody?

    A. setting aside timed oral reading each day

    B. modeling an appropriate reading rate

    C. using ability grouping for silent reading

    D. having students act out a play from a script

ANSWER KEY

1) **A.** This sorting exercise helps students identify both letter sounds and the initial sounds of words.

2) **D.** Sight words should be memorized for instant recognition to aid in automaticity.

3) **C.** The word *sign* deviates from standard phonics structures. The fact that the /g/ is not pronounced and the /i/ is a long vowel sound must simply be memorized.

4) **A.** One of the disadvantages of this method is that more complex words cannot be spelled phonetically.

5) **B.** Asking about the sounds the letters make will help the student decode the word *woods* by sounding it out.

6) **A.** The word *dirt* contains an *r*-controlled vowel, which is one of the most challenging structures.

7) **D.** *Miser* contains both an open syllable and an *r*-controlled vowel: *Mi* (open syllable) *ser* (*r*-controlled vowel).

8) **A.** Reading a broad array of books builds background knowledge, which can then be applied and

9) **C.** This exercise helps the student to use the sentence's structure to determine that the word *Istanbul* must be a place.

10) **C.** In semantic impressions, students write a story with the words from the text.

11) **D.** Most dictionaries include an entry for the word *origin* that students should be taught to use.

12) **D.** Having students read from a script would give them practice reading expressively.

3. Comprehension of Literary and Informational Text

Comprehension

Developing Listening and Speaking Skills

Listening and speaking skills and the development of reading skills are entwined in children from a young age. Children who understand the role of oral language in communication and how to produce and "consume" oral language will have a head start in learning to read.

From a young age, children should be encouraged to have conversations with adults and peers as much as possible. Such interactions help children understand the role of oral language in communications. Conversations also show them the best way to use oral language to express needs or preferences, to join a group in play, or to pretend to exist in another world (imaginative play).

Vocabulary development can also be encouraged in young children or English learners through **picture vocabulary cards**, which can then serve as a springboard to incorporate new words into the classroom in both speaking and listening. Listening to and singing songs and rhymes can also aid in both vocabulary development and phonemic awareness. **Guided storybook reading** and whole-group activities that require students to speak and listen, such as **show-and-tell**, also aid in oral language development of young learners.

As students become more proficient with oral language in an organic context, various targeted instructional strategies can aid in development of these skills.

▶ "think-pair-share" activities in which students first think of an idea or opinion about a topic, then pair up with another student or group, and finally share this idea

▶ "ask three then me" activities in which students ask three peers to try to answer a question before asking for the teacher's help

▶ peer tutoring

▶ flexible grouping

▶ collaborative learning

▶ role-play/dramatizations/impromptu dialogues

▶ oral presentations/speeches

▶ debates

▶ discussions

▶ oral reading/recitation

When planning oral language activities, it is helpful to consider the particular skills being targeted. For example, a teacher might want to encourage students to develop prosody as they recite or read a poem

or monologue to the class. Another activity might be aimed at having students use oral language in a pragmatic context by first considering audience before planning a speech or oral presentation.

Listening skills can be slower to develop, especially among young children. However, games like Simon Says and others in which students must follow oral directions can be useful and enjoyable. A popular technique with elementary students is **whole body listening**. This strategy gives students explicit instruction in how to listen with their entire body.

▶ eyes should be on the speaker

▶ ears should be listening

▶ mouth should be quiet

▶ hands should be in the lap or away from others

▶ feet should be still

▶ body should be pointed toward the speaker

▶ brain should be thinking about what it is hearing

▶ heart should be considerate of others

Depending on the student age and context, **active listening** skills can also be taught. Active listening, or reflective listening, describes students' ability to repeat what has been said to check for understanding. Students can use active listening strategies in several ways: asking questions after hearing a speaker or lecture, taking notes that summarize what the speaker has said, and using verbal or nonverbal affirmations of understanding as the person is speaking.

Sample Question

1) A reading and language arts teacher is planning a unit on listening skills for fourth graders. Which activity would MOST appropriate?
   A. having students memorize and recite poetry in front of the teacher for a grade based on inflection and accuracy
   B. having a guest speaker visit the classroom to discuss a topic and answer student questions
   C. having students watch a video and then ask questions about parts they did not understand
   D. having students find a solution to a school-wide problem that affects them all

Oral Language for Critical Thinking and Creative Expression

Students should also be expected to use oral language to think critically and communicate their thoughts. This process relies on both **receptive oral language**, the ability to understand what is being said, and **expressive oral language**, the ability to use language to communicate ideas appropriately.

Techniques for developing oral language skills for critical thinking and creative expression vary by age level. Strategies for younger students include:

▶ asking students to describe objects in the room or that they see out the window or outside on a nature walk

▶ asking students to describe how two objects or pictures are similar or different

▶ encouraging play with props in the dramatic play center

- encouraging students to pretend to be a character from a story

- asking students to describe another person or themselves aloud

Techniques for developing oral language skills for critical thinking and creative expression for older students include:

- oral discussion or critiques of literature or expository texts

- reciprocal teaching (students become the teachers and guide a small-group reading activity)

- "book club" or book discussion activities in large or small groups

- oral discussions with peers on current events or issues that require critical reflection

- persuasive speeches or presentations

- plays or dramatic performances

- writing and reading a piece of creative writing aloud

- impromptu dialogues or role-plays

Sample Question

2) An upper elementary teacher wants to incorporate a critical speaking and listening activity into a unit in which students read a play that ends tragically. Which instructional strategy best meets this goal?
   A. filling out a graphic organizer before, during, and after reading the play
   B. reading the play aloud with dramatic inflection
   C. holding a class-wide debate on whose fault the tragedy really was
   D. encouraging students to use fix-it-up strategies as they read the tragedy orally

Reading Comprehension Foundations

Reading comprehension does not happen in a vacuum. It exists in combination with other processes. Reading comprehension is built on three foundations:

▶ **Linguistic foundations** describe the way written and oral language are involved in the reading process. Students with a strong background in the basics of the English language will generally have much stronger comprehension of texts.

▶ **Sociological or cultural foundations** describe the way readers approach the reading task based on their unique environment and cultural constructs. Readers come from different backgrounds that will guide their approach. Teachers should respect and facilitate this with a variety of approaches.

▶ **Psychological or cognitive foundations** describe how the brain works during the reading process. Examples include how the eye and brain work together to make meaning of texts, and how the brain processes and stores such information for recall.

Check Your Understanding

What are some assessment tools or techniques that could help a teacher determine a child's current linguistic foundation?

These processes inform how each student will experience the process of learning to read and how the process must be differentiated for all readers. For example, a student with few oral language skills will find reading more challenging than a student with oral language skills. A student from an environment that does not value reading as a worthwhile

leisure activity may not be interested in learning to read at first. A student with a cognitive disability such as Down syndrome may need extra help to recall what has been read.

Reading is also a very connected process. Hollis Scarborough calls this the strands of the **reading rope**. This rope has two major parts: **language comprehension** and **word recognition**. Language comprehension includes background and vocabulary knowledge, knowledge of language structure, literacy knowledge, and verbal reasoning. Word recognition includes phonological awareness, decoding, and sight recognition. Developing skills in word recognition makes reading **increasingly automatic**, and developing skills in language comprehension makes reading **increasingly strategic**. All of this weaves together into the act of skilled reading.

A related theory was proposed by Linnea Ehri and involves four phases of how children learn to read words.

1. In the **pre-alphabetic phase**, children can identify words based on memorization, picture cues, or guessing. For example, students may know the sign says "McDonalds," even though they cannot technically 'read' the word.

2. In the **partial alphabetic phase**, students have some knowledge of letter-sound correspondence, which they use, though often incorrectly. For example, students may see the word "dog" and recognize /g/, so say the word is "grape." Or, they may have learned that "apple" starts with /a/, so they may say "apple" for any word that begins with /a/.

3. In the **full alphabetic phase**, students have mastered letter-sound correspondence, so they sound out the sound of each letter. This may be clunky. For example, children may sound out "balloon" as b-a-l-l-o-o-n.

4. The **consolidated alphabetic phase** involves use of bigger chunks instead of individual letters. They may recognize phonics patterns like digraphs or suffixes. However, they may still be likely to segment some parts of words such as ch/eeze.

5. The last phase is the **automatic phase** wherein most words are instantly recognized by sight. When new words are encountered, the reader can use strategies to quickly decode them. This is the phase most fluent readers have mastered.

Teachers should understand the transactional nature of reading a text and provide students with ongoing, systematic instruction in a variety of reading strategies to equip their students to become active readers. **Active readers** get involved with a text by making connections between their **background knowledge** (what they already know) and what they are learning or experiencing. They seek meaning in what they read in order to solve a problem, to gain new knowledge, or to answer a question about something that matters to them. Teachers can instill active reading skills in their students throughout the reading process—before, during, and after reading.

Sample Question

3) Which strategy can be employed to help students activate background knowledge before they read a text?
   A. reciprocal teaching
   B. the Frayer Model
   C. OPIN
   D. K-W-L Chart

Strategies for Comprehension

Teachers should model and practice pre-reading strategies throughout reading instruction, before beginning each new text. One such strategy is **previewing** a text, which involves identifying the author, the genre, and the general subject matter before reading the text. It also includes reading headings and chapter titles, examining related graphics, researching the author and the context of the work (as age-appropriate), and anticipating the author's purpose.

Previewing general information about a text allows an active reader to use another pre-reading strategy: **setting a purpose**. A teacher might introduce each new text with a guiding question (What does it mean to be evil?) or a hypothetical situation that pushes students to examine their own value systems (Imagine you are a business owner. Should you be required to hire a certain number of individuals with disabilities?).

After facilitating a discussion about the question or scenario, the teacher directs students to a particular text to examine how the author or characters would respond. By setting a purpose for students' reading, the teacher is guiding them toward the thematic elements of the text. Students are encouraged to draw connections between the author's choices and the overall message.

Before reading a new text, and throughout the reading process, students should also make predictions about what they are reading. A **prediction** is a kind of inference that is concerned with what is going to happen next in a text. Making predictions is a valuable active reading skill because it requires readers to be constantly aware of what is going on in the text and what the author may be foreshadowing through their specific choices.

In addition to making predictions as they read, students should be thinking about their own level of understanding, also known as metacognition. In **metacognition**, readers think about what they are thinking as they read. This helps to immediately identify any confusion or uncertainty. Readers who are aware of their thought processes are able to recognize and react when understanding breaks down.

Part of metacognition in reading is using **fix-up** or **fix-it-up strategies**. Active readers apply these strategies when they realize they do not understand what they are reading. Common fix-up strategies include:

- ▶ slowing down the reading pace
- ▶ rereading the section in question
- ▶ reading beyond the text in question to see if confusion is cleared up
- ▶ using text clues
- ▶ illustrations/graphic elements
- ▶ text features (bold words, italics, headings, relevant punctuation)
- ▶ figuring out the meaning of unfamiliar words
  - using context clues/words around the confusing word
  - using picture clues
  - using a resource to look up the word or words
- ▶ asking a peer or teacher for assistance

Annotating is another important strategy that takes place during reading. To provide effective instruction in annotation and ensure that students are mastering the skill, teachers should set clear guidelines and expectations. For example, a teacher might ask students to make VISA annotations. **VISA annotations** involve noting interesting or new <u>v</u>ocabulary, important <u>i</u>nferences, helpful <u>s</u>ummaries, and brief <u>a</u>nalyses.

Other annotating strategies include:

▶ underlining or highlighting main ideas or important information

▶ circling key words

▶ placing question marks next to confusing parts that might need further attention

▶ writing notes in the margins

Questioning is another way students can develop overall comprehension of a text. The reader asks and then answers questions about what has been read. Questioning occurs on three levels.

1. Literal questions are based on explicit information in the text and require only recall or identification of information from the text.

"On what day did Mark send the letter?"

2. **Inferential questions** are based on implicit information in the text. These questions require students to make an inference or prediction or to draw a conclusion.

"What will Mark most likely do after he sends the letter?"

3. **Evaluative questions** require readers to form an opinion on the text. Students will need to understand explicit information and then consider how they feel about this information.

"What do I think about Mark's action in sending the letter?"

Summarization is a reading strategy to help readers determine what is important in the text. Using their own words, readers reduce a text or section of text to its main points or central ideas. Students do this by skipping insignificant details and redundancies and looking for general ideas rather than specific facts and examples.

Student-produced summaries can provide valuable insight into comprehension levels. Students who actively comprehend what they read will produce accurate summaries. Those who struggle with comprehension may leave out important ideas or leave in unnecessary information. Summaries should be used throughout the study of a text and in the post-reading process to gauge how well students understood the basic ideas of the work.

Teachers can encourage students to engage with the text using other post-reading strategies, such as having them **reflect** on their experience of the text and write formal or informal responses. They may also ask students to return to the guiding question, synthesizing their understanding of the text and its thematic and cultural relevance. Students can also **make connections** between the text, themselves (text-to-self), the world (text-to-world), and other literature (text-to-text).

Students should be encouraged to use **text evidence** in any post-reading exercise, even in their personal responses. It is important that their conclusions and understandings are fully informed and truly based in the text itself. In fact, as readers consider textual evidence, they may change or expand their original interpretations. Examination of textual evidence is an essential part of the process of constructing meaning.

Sample Question

4) A teacher is working with a small group of fourth-grade students receiving Tier 2 interventions aimed at improving comprehension. Which technique is the teacher MOST likely to recommend to students?
- A. using graphophonic cues
- B. applying fix-up strategies
- C. coarticulation of phonemes
- D. moving tiles in Elkonin boxes

Independent Reading Strategies

While teachers will be explicitly teaching various comprehension strategies, it is vital that students **read independently** without scaffolding. Research shows that students who read independently have better educational outcomes in almost every area. When students read independently, they must apply all the active reading strategies they learn in the classroom in an authentic context.

Unfortunately, research also shows that many children neither engage in nor enjoy independent reading. These students will need extra encouragement from educators to read independently. Following are some strategies to promote independent reading in various settings and grade levels.

▶ **Daily reading logs** can be used in or outside of school. Many elementary and middle schools require at least fifteen minutes per day.

▶ Formal independent reading programs like **Sustained Silent Reading (SSR)** or **Drop Everything and Read (DEAR)** can be used on a school or classroom level.

▶ Classrooms can be stocked with **lending libraries** full of books that teachers enthusiastically recommend to students.

▶ Educators can recommend books based on student interests. Resources like annotated bibliographies organized by topic and Lexile/grade level as well as digital applications that match books to interests and reading level can be very helpful.

▶ Frequent use of the school library can promote student desire for independent reading. Educators can help scaffold book selection by guiding students to relevant material.

▶ **Book clubs** and **book discussion groups** can be particularly effective, especially among older students. The accountability factor of reading the book before the meeting can be a strong motivation to read independently.

▶ Independent reading can be promoted across the school's digital community. School social media sites might encourage a #nowreading hashtag or encourage students and parents to post book recommendations. School or teacher websites can include curated booklists or summer reading lists.

Sample Question

5) After conducting a survey, reading teacher discovers that only 12 percent of students are reading independently at home outside of reading for homework assignments. How might the teacher MOST effectively address this situation?

A. assign more self-directed reading comprehension exercises

B. conduct additional research to find out why students do not enjoy reading for pleasure

C. start a program that rewards students for completing independent reading logs each week

D. send home literature with students that describes current research on the importance of independent reading

Text Complexity

Finding a balance between the complexity of a text and a student's level of literacy development can be challenging. Many programs recognize this challenge and structure goal-setting and student assessments in a growth-over-time approach. Regardless of the milestones laid out by a school or district, teachers should encourage students to tackle ever-more sophisticated texts as they develop the foundational skills they need to take on new challenges. However, this does not mean pushing students beyond what they can decode. Giving students developmentally inappropriate texts may lead to a lack of confidence and less interest in and enthusiasm for reading.

Many factors contribute to a text's complexity. In determining appropriateness, educators should evaluate texts based on both qualitative and quantitative measures and their match to the reader. **Quantitative measurements** include anything for which a number can be calculated, such as word frequency, length of words and sentence length, average syllables per word, and so on.

Quantitative measurements can calculate a range or score that is assigned to a text. For example, **MetaMetrics** is a company that uses word frequency and sentence length in an equation to yield a score. Scores are assigned to both readers and texts. Those assigned to readers typically come from standardized tests and measure current level of reading ability; these are called **reader measures**.

> **Did You Know?**
>
> MetaMetrics also offers Lexile measures for Spanish-language texts.

MetaMetrics also assigns **Lexile ranges** to texts called Lexile text measures or Lexile measures. While these ranges do not have a direct correlation to grade level, educators can use charts created by MetaMetrics and/or a state or district to find the typical Lexile ranges for a given grade. The company states that the best results come from a reader measure that falls within a "sweet spot" range per the text measure.

> **Helpful Hint**
>
> Lexile measures are only effective for texts that follow a typical structure. They are not effective for poetry and drama—these types of texts must be measured for complexity using other methods.

Most of what students read (textbooks, passages in software programs, published children's literature) has already been assigned a Lexile text measure. Teachers can raise students' chances of enjoyment and comprehension of texts by ensuring that the Lexile text measure fits within the average range for the grade level and, more importantly, for each student's reader measure.

Grade	Reader Measures, Midyear **25th to 75th Percentile** This is the typical range of reading ability for students in each grade. These measures are designed to help compare a student's level to a typical range; they are not intended to be standards.	Text Measures These text measures have been revised from previous measures to better align with the Common Core State Standards for English Language Arts to ensure that students will meet these standards and be "college and career ready" by the end of high school.
1	BR120L to 295L	190L to 530L
2	170L to 545L	420L to 650L
3	415L to 760L	520L to 820L
4	635L to 950L	740L to 940L
5	770L to 1080L	830L to 1010L
6	855L to 1165L	925L to 1070L
7	925L to 1235L	970L to 1120L
8	985L to 1295L	1010L to 1185L
9	1040L to 1350L	1050L to 1260L
10	1085L to 1400L	1080L to 1335L
11 and 12	1130L to 1440L	1185L to 1385L

Table 3.1. Lexile Reader and Text Measures for Grades 1 – 12

Other metrics for measuring the readability of a text include scales such as the **Flesch–Kincaid Grade Level**, or ATOS level. A specific program or school may also use another proprietary tool such as Accelerated Reader Bookfinder or Scholastic Book Levels.

Beyond the quantitative measures determined by Lexile and others are qualitative measures, such as:

▶ the layout of the text: illustrations, text size

▶ the overall text structure: simple narrative chronology, more advanced argumentative essay

▶ sentence structure: prevalence of simple or more complex sentences

▶ levels of meaning: whether ideas are explicitly or implicitly communicated

▶ knowledge demand: the cultural knowledge or other ideas that the reader must already know

The overall language and vocabulary of the text also generally fall under qualitative measures, although some quantitative scales measure the frequency of vocabulary that students of a particular age or grade are not likely to be familiar with.

Sample Question

6) What is the BEST way to differentiate instruction in a first-grade reading classroom?
   A. practice oral reading with only the more advanced students so those struggling will not feel uncomfortable
   B. use only texts on the lower end of the first-grade Lexile range to ensure they are accessible to all students
   C. set aside time for students to engage in silent reading with a teacher-selected book based on student ability and interests
   D. conduct additional phonics drills with students who need help with decoding while the other students do a science experiment

Selecting Texts

No single measure of any text can determine appropriateness for all students. For example, Lexile ranges do not account for mature subject matter. Teachers also need to differentiate literacy instruction in the classroom. While literacy development requires reading more and more complex texts, students do not benefit from inaccessible reading material. In fact, this can lead to bad habits such as guessing at or skipping unfamiliar words instead of trying to decode and asking for help before figuring out an unfamiliar word or text.

Whatever strategy a program uses to address individualization of reading instruction (pull-out, push-in, small groups, intervention teacher, etc.), teachers must find a just-right level of text complexity where students are challenged but not frustrated. Text complexity is highly individualized and should be matched to the instructional task:

▶ Texts at the **independent reading level** (for independent reading) require students to read with 99 percent accuracy and 90 percent comprehension. These are generally texts just "below" a student's reading level.

▶ **Instructional reading level** texts are used for teacher-guided instruction and are typically read at 85 percent accuracy with over 75 percent comprehension. These texts are usually "at" the student's reading level.

▶ **Frustration level** texts are those read at less than 85 percent accuracy and less than 50 percent comprehension. These texts are generally "above" a student's reading level and are not recommended. New research, however, suggests such texts might be effective in paired reading activities with proficient readers.

In addition to selecting texts based on text measures, educators should consider other factors that depend on age. These are good questions to ask when selecting appropriate texts for early-childhood classroom instruction:

▶ Does the text introduce or reinforce concepts introduced in the curriculum (sight word acquisition, phonemic awareness, letter sounds, etc.)?

▶ Does the text have picture/text correlation that will hold readers' attention and provide comprehension clues?

▶ Does the text teach an important lesson or moral?

▶ Are the characters and situations diverse and engaging?

The following questions should guide the selection of texts for students:

▶ Are texts aligned to instructional goals?

▶ Are texts at the appropriate level (instructional or independent) for the planned activity?

▶ Are texts relevant and aligned to student interests?

▶ Do texts promote deep comprehension or analysis?

▶ Do texts contain highly specialized or nuanced vocabulary that students may not be familiar with?

▶ Do texts offer **multimodal elements** (appealing to different modes of communication such as written text, spoken language, and visual images) that might be relevant for instructional objectives?

When students are **self-selecting texts** or choosing something to read based on their own interests, they may still need scaffolding from educators. Knowing a student's personality, interests, and independent reading level can be helpful in this regard. However, even independent reading levels can evolve. Some students may seek out and enjoy more challenging texts, while others become frustrated at that level. Knowledge of the individual student should guide suggestions.

As teachers guide students both by selecting appropriate texts for students and helping students select them on their own, an eye toward motivation and engagement should be ever-present. Additionally, text should be culturally responsive, or should reflect the myriad cultures of students in order to validate the value of all backgrounds. Further, while print books are often the norm in certain settings, digital texts often have an array of built-in features like annotation tools and dictionaries that can benefit many students. Students should be exposed to both print and digital texts to the extent possible.

Sample Question

7) One disadvantage of relying on Lexile level as the sole indicator of text appropriateness is that
   A. it is only applicable to students whose first language is English.
   B. it fails to account for qualitative text features.
   C. it does not encourage the reading of rigorous texts.
   D. it can only be used to measure fiction texts.

Building Comprehension of Fiction

Readers of all ages usually enjoy fiction texts, thanks to relatable characters and well-developed plots. Teachers often use familiar stories as a springboard to more in-depth comprehension because students are familiar with the literal meaning of the text. For this reason, many readings of the same story in an early childhood classroom are not uncommon.

Reading several interpretations of a familiar story such as *Cinderella* from different cultural perspectives can allow students to apply background knowledge of a familiar tale in new contexts. While there are many specific strategies to aid students in comprehension of literary texts, some of the most common include:

Using Graphic or Semantic Organizers

▶ storyboards or event sequence frames or timelines

▶ story maps (beginning, middle, end) or plot diagrams (rising action, climax, falling action, resolution)

► character maps (actions, feelings, appearance, dialogue)

► character trait identification charts

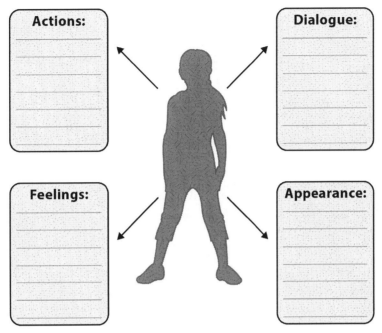

Figure 3.2. Character Map

Guided Comprehension Questions

► those requiring students to underline, highlight, and locate the answer in the text

► those requiring a constructed response

► cloze exercises in which a portion of the text is removed and readers must fill in the blanks

Summarization and Main Idea Exercises

► written retellings that ask students to recall and write down important parts of the story in their own words

► exercises that ask students to create an outline of the story

► asking students to identify main or central ideas in the story

► asking students to identify themes or messages within the story

Specific Targeted Strategies

► **Directed Reading-Thinking Activity (DR-TA)**: Students make predictions and read up to a preselected stopping point. They then evaluate and refine predictions based on text evidence.

► The **QAR Strategy** encourages students to identify the type of question and to think about *how* to find the answer.

- ▪ "Right There" questions are literal questions that require only the location of the relevant part.

- ▪ "Think and Search" questions require synthesis from multiple parts of the text.

- "Author and You" questions require the text to have been read, but the answer is not directly in the text. They are typically inference and depth of knowledge (DOK) 2 and 3 questions.

- "On My Own" questions require background knowledge and do not rely on text evidence directly.

▶ The **SQ3R strategy** was developed for reading textbooks, but it is useful for many different reading materials.

- **S**urvey: previewing the text and taking note of graphics, headings, etc.

- **Q**uestion: generating questions about the text after previewing

- **R**ead: reading and looking for answers for the questions

- **R**ecite: rehearsing or saying the answers to the questions

- **R**eview: reviewing text and answering or responding to any other questions

Group or Paired Strategies

▶ **Reciprocal teaching** assigns roles to groups of four students who together work to read and comprehend a text.

▶ **Think-pair-share** pairs students to answer comprehension questions about a text. First, students think about their own answer, activating background knowledge. They then pair with another student or a small group. Then they share their answer with their group or partner and then the entire class.

▶ **Peer-Assisted Learning Strategies (PALS)**, a student partners with a classmate. They take turns providing each other assistance and feedback in reading comprehension.

> **Check Your Understanding**
>
> Practice using the SQ3R strategy for the next chapter of this text. Did you find it useful? Which grade levels and types of texts do you think it would be most useful for in your current or future practice?

Sample Question

8) A teacher plans to structure independent practice in a classroom with students of various skill levels. How should the teacher proceed?
   A. focus instruction on pragmatics so that students see the connections in what they are learning
   B. switch to an analogy-based phonics method of instruction to engage all students
   C. use running records to keep track of student progress and current skill level
   D. implement Peer-Assisted Learning Strategies (PALS) as appropriate to provide scaffolding

Literary Genres

Literature can be classified into **genres** and subgenres, categories of works that are similar in format, content, tone, or length. Most works fall into one of four broad genres: nonfiction, fiction, drama, and poetry.

As students experience each genre throughout a school year, they should receive instruction that integrates all aspects of literacy. That is, students should not only experience reading practice in each

genre; they should also have plenty of writing and discussion practice to deepen their knowledge of the genre they are studying.

Fiction

Fiction is a prose genre. Texts are made up of narratives created by the author. Fiction is typically written in the form of novels and short stories. Many subgenres fall under the category of fiction. Students can be guided to determine whether a text is fiction or nonfiction by asking whether the text is a "true" or "real" story.

Folklore is a set of beliefs and stories of a particular people, which are passed down through the generations. Folklore comes in many forms, including:

▶ fables: short stories intended to teach moral lessons

▶ fairy tales: stories that involve magical creatures such as elves and fairies

▶ myths: stories, often involving gods or demigods, that attempt to explain certain practices or phenomena

▶ legends: unverifiable stories that seem to have a degree of realism about them

▶ tall tales: stories that are set in realistic settings but include characters with wildly exaggerated capabilities

Students can be guided to identify folklore by asking certain questions about texts:

▶ Are there supernatural elements, such as magic, dragons, or fairies?

▶ Does the story teach a lesson?

▶ Do the characters in the stories have exaggerated abilities?

▶ Is the story from a particular cultural tradition?

Science fiction is a category of fiction in which writers tell imaginative stories that are grounded in scientific and technological theories or realities. Science fiction writing often explores ideas involving the future of humanity and its relationship with the universe or with technology. A subcategory of science fiction is dystopian fiction, in which authors explore social, cultural, and political structures in the context of a futuristic world.

Horror fiction is intended to frighten, startle, or disgust the reader. Often, horror fiction involves paranormal or psychological content. Mysteries and thrillers, which may also arouse fear or paranoia, tend to be fast-paced and outcome-driven; they also tend to focus on human behaviors or relationships and not on paranormal activity.

Realistic fiction is meant to be relatable for readers. Authors of realistic fiction try to create a degree of verisimilitude in their writing, especially in the dialogue between characters. **Historical fiction** relies on realistic settings and characters from an earlier time to tell new stories. Often the setting is central to the motivations and actions of characters. Students might need to explore the background of a historical era before they can comprehend a historical fiction text at the highest level.

Satire is a literary text that uses critical humor to reveal vice and foolishness in individuals and institutions. The purpose of satire is to somehow improve the object of ridicule. The literary or rhetorical devices that create satire include sarcasm, irony, mockery, exaggeration, understatement, as well as an honest narrative/speaking voice that is dismayed or appalled by the object of the satire.

Because satire is a complex literary device that requires comprehension well beyond a literal or even basic inferential level, it is regarded as a more challenging type of text reserved for older students and more advanced readers.

Sample Question

9) A teacher is working with a second-grade student receiving Tier 3 interventions in fluency and decoding. Before the day's activity, which will involve reading from a leveled reader, the teacher asks the student to preview the booklet's title and illustrations and make a prediction about the type of book it is. This helps the student to
- A. develop metacognition.
- B. apply fix-up strategies.
- C. determine genre.
- D. analyze plot.

Drama

Drama is expressive writing that tells a story to an audience through the actions and dialogue of characters, which are brought to life by actors who play the roles onstage. Dramatic works, called **plays**, are written in poetic or lyrical verse or in regular prose. Along with the dialogue between the characters, authors rely on **stage directions** to describe the sets and to give directions to the actors about what they are to do.

In some plays, actors perform long speeches in which the characters explain their thinking about philosophical ideas or social issues. These **monologues** can be directed toward another character. A monologue delivered as if nobody were listening is called a **soliloquy** (as in Shakespeare's famous "To be or not to be" soliloquy from *Hamlet*). Sometimes characters in drama (or fiction) have very unique attributes such as a manner of speech, dress, or a catchphrase. Such devices make characters memorable to readers and are known as **character tags**.

Using drama in the classroom is a great way to get students interested in different types of texts. A simple stage in a kindergarten or elementary classroom is a natural outgrowth of a dramatic play center sometimes found in preschool classrooms. Building on students' innate curiosity and imagination, the possibilities are endless. Acting out dramas not only helps students work on expressive reading (prosody); it also reinforces social and emotional learning as students analyze the emotions and actions of characters.

It is important to have older students think about how both the stage directions and the dialogue contribute to the play's meaning. To jog student interest, especially in linguistically complex dramas like those of Shakespeare, teachers might have students watch video clips of actual performances. Comparing specific scenes performed by different actors stimulates interest and can be used to discuss the different ways a scene can be interpreted.

Students may also benefit from acting out scenes or giving speeches, allowing them to express their own interpretations of the characters or action. To engage students in writing activities, a teacher may have them write their own scripts or write a research report on the play's context, author, characters, or subject matter.

Sample Question

10) Drama is a genre well suited for helping students develop
    A. phonemic awareness.
    B. prosody.
    C. alliteration.
    D. concepts of print.

Poetry

Poetry is imaginative, expressive verse writing that uses rhythm, unified and concentrated thought, concrete images, specialized language, and patterns. Different poetic forms use techniques and structures in unique ways.

A **line** is a unit of poetry. The lines of a poem can be separated by punctuation, meter, and/or rhyme. Although a line may be a unit of attention, it is usually not a unit of meaning.

A **stanza** is a group of lines followed by a space. Each stanza of a poem may have a specific number of lines; the lines are sometimes arranged in a pattern created by meter and/or a rhyme scheme. The pattern is often repeated in each stanza, although it can be varied for effect. A stanza with two lines is a **couplet**; three lines, a **tercet**; four lines, a **quatrain**; five lines, a **cinquain**; and so on. Modern poems may have stanzas with varying lengths or no stanzas at all. Some modern poems are written entirely in **free verse**, without any fixed form.

Teachers can introduce several common types of poems to students during reading instruction:

▶ A **ballad** is a short narrative song about an event that is considered important. Ballads are intended to be recited. They are characterized by a dramatic immediacy, focusing on one crucial situation or action that often leads to a catastrophe.

▶ A **sonnet** is a lyrical poem with fourteen lines, usually written in **iambic pentameter**. This pattern alternates stressed and unstressed syllables in a line of verse with ten syllables per line.

▶ A **haiku** is a short poem format that originated in Japan. It has three lines of five, seven, and five syllables.

▶ A **villanelle** is usually nineteen lines long. It has five stanzas, each with three lines, and a final stanza of four lines. It includes a refrain—two lines that repeat throughout the poem following a specific pattern.

Teachers can use poetry lessons as ways for students to respond both to the effect the poem had on them personally and to the aesthetics of the poem itself. To introduce poetry and build interest for a poetry unit, a teacher might select an especially forceful poem, read it dramatically, and invite students to discuss their responses.

When students are analyzing a poem, it is important to read it more than once. The teacher can model with a **think-aloud**, the process of modeling one's thinking during a reading. Students should have copies of poems to annotate and have a routine for collaborative and independent poetry reading, such as:

1. an initial reading to experience the mood of the poem and the musicality of the language

2. a second reading to focus on the pauses and thought units and to identify the **speaker**, who may not be the same person as the poet

3. a third close reading to take marginal notes on the structure of the poem, the denotation (literal meaning) and connotations (subtle meanings) of unfamiliar words, the impact of imagery and figurative language, and the meaning of confusing lines or phrases

4. a final reading to come up with some thematic ideas, drawn from the details

Along with analyzing poems, students can present their original poetry in classroom "coffee houses" or "poetry slams." Depending on the age and grade, students might learn different poetic forms, like sonnets and ballads. They might also learn about the characteristics of the different types of poetry, including metaphysical poetry or Romantic poetry.

While poetry analysis may be associated with older children, even young students can appreciate and recognize rhyme. Poetry with **rhyme** can help reinforce phonological awareness and is a natural outgrowth of many young children's love of song. **Meter**—the rhythm, or beat, of the poem—can also engage young students with different texts. A beat can be clapped to, stomped to, or even danced to. Many timeless books for children—such as *One Fish, Two Fish, Red Fish, Blue Fish* and *Each Peach Pear Plum*—have both rhyme and meter and expose young children to poetry in a fun way.

Young writers may even begin to write simple poems with one or two stanzas, or groups of lines similar to paragraphs. Students should be encouraged to recognize and create their own rhyming words as an additional outgrowth of phonological awareness. Asking students to name all the words they can think of that rhyme with *dog*, for example, will allow for continued practice with rhymes.

> ### Check Your Understanding
>
> Lexile text measures are not used for poetry. Create a list of qualitative text features that could determine the appropriateness of a poem for a grade level or group of students.

Poetry often uses **figurative language**, or phrases not meant to be interpreted literally. A simile compares two things of a different type ("brave like a lion"). A metaphor applies a characteristic or meaning to an object or action that is not literally applicable ("the anger of the rose stung us with its sharp fury"). Poems may also use **sensory imagery**, or descriptive language that appeals to one of the five senses ("the shrill cry of the alarm"). **Alliteration** is the repetition of the same sound in nearby words ("the rotund rhinoceros roared").

Teaching non-literal language can be a challenge for students, especially young students who may think concretely. However, certain instructional strategies are recommended:

➤ Use direct instruction to introduce the types of figurative language such as simile and metaphor

➤ Use mentor texts with strong and accessible figurative language

➤ Help students identify figurative language in texts as well as the author's most likely purpose for its use

➤ Encourage students to reflect on the impact of figurative language on the reader and how the text would have been different without it

➤ Incorporate figurative language into writing assignments whenever possible to increase exposure

Sample Question

11) A reading teacher is planning a lesson on rhyme and meter in poetry for a student with a specific reading disability. Which assistive technology could be useful?
- A. an e-reader or digital copy of the poem
- B. an audio recording of the poem
- C. a large-print version of the poem
- D. a version of the poem adapted at a lower Lexile level

Literary Response and Analysis

The **structural elements** of literature such as setting, characters, conflict, tone, point of view, main idea, and organization can be introduced with other literacy activities, even with students who are pre-readers.

Setting and Character

Setting is the time and place of events in a story. When considering setting, students should look at how characters interact with their surroundings, how they are influenced by the societal expectations of that time and place, and how the location and time period impact the development of the story. Students might have trouble understanding the difference between setting and plot. Teachers can ask, "How would this story change if it were set in a different time or place?" to help students understand setting.

An author uses **character development** to create characters that are complex and, to some degree, believable. Authors might develop their characters directly by telling the reader explicitly what the character is like by describing traits and values. Sometimes, authors include the thoughts and feelings of the characters themselves, offering readers even more insight. Authors also develop their characters indirectly by revealing their actions and interactions with others. They might do this by including what one character says or thinks about another and allowing readers to draw their own conclusions. Most authors combine direct and indirect characterization. This ensures that readers know what they need to know and provides opportunities for reflection and interpretation.

Sample Question

12) A third grade teacher wants to model inferencing strategies while reading a fictional text that develops a single character in detail. Which strategy is most appropriate?
- A. drawing a plot pyramid
- B. filling in a KWL chart
- C. conducting a think aloud
- D. showing fix up strategies

Tone

The **tone** of a literary work is created by the author's attitude toward the reader and the subject of the text. In a sense, it is the tone of voice the author uses to speak to the reader. Depending on word choice, an author's tone can range from playful, familiar, or sincere to detached, sarcastic, or indifferent. It can be alarmed and forceful or philosophical and serious. It might be concerned or careless, saddened or overjoyed, triumphant or defeated.

Whatever the case, students should be encouraged to consider how the author uses language to convey tone. Students can think about what the author is suggesting through language choice. This process will reveal the author's attitude and, ultimately, the theme of the work.

Students should also be able to distinguish the author's tone from **mood**. Mood is the emotional atmosphere of a literary work that shapes the reader's experience of the text. Mood is created through an interplay of the literary elements of plot, character, setting, point of view, tone, and figurative language. By examining the emotional effect of the author's choices, readers can further develop their understanding of the text's larger meaning.

Sample Question

13) Which of the following strategies would BEST help a student identify the tone of a literary work?
   A.   implementing pre-reading strategies like previewing, scanning, and predicting
   B.   using a list-group-label process to dig deeper into key concepts from the work
   C.   focusing on the morphology and orthography of words found in the text
   D.   identifying specific words in the text that evoke feelings or emotions

Point of View

Point of view is the perspective from which the action in a story is told. By carefully selecting a particular point of view, writers are able to control what their readers know. Most literature is written in first-person or third-person point of view. In the **first-person** or "I" point of view, the action is narrated by a character within the story. This can make the story feel more believable and authentic to the reader. However, the reader's knowledge and understanding are limited to what the narrator notices and are influenced by what the narrator thinks and values.

A **third-person** narrator is a voice outside the action of the story, an observer who shares what he or she knows, sees, or hears with the reader. A third-person narrator might be fully omniscient (able to see into the minds of the characters and share what they are thinking and feeling), partially omniscient (able to see into the minds of just one or a few characters), or limited (unable to see into the minds of any of the characters and only able to share what can be seen and heard).

The **second-person** point of view uses "you" and can be read as the narrator speaking directly to the reader. It is used mainly in nonfiction texts, particularly in introductory and concluding paragraphs in which the writer might make a direct appeal to the reader to reflect on the points about to be made or already made.

Students can learn to associate certain pronouns with certain points of view if such an exercise is developmentally appropriate. For example, teachers might ask very young students questions like "Who told the story?" and "What was (character name) like?" to introduce these concepts.

Although point of view may be harder for very young students to grasp, teachers can begin introducing the basic concept by reading the narrator's part in one voice and each different character in a different voice and encouraging students to do the same. Older students can practice second-person point of view by reading and writing letters to other students, the teacher, or administrators or other school personnel.

Sample Question

14) An upper elementary teacher is working on an integrated reading and writing unit on point of view. He wants to expose students to multiple perspectives in texts but discourage them from using the pronoun "you" in formal academic writing. The teacher would most likely NOT assign which writing task?
- A. personal narrative
- B. research report
- C. formal letter
- D. compare/contrast essay

Main Idea and Theme

As students progress in their literacy and are able to consistently decode longer passages, their focus will shift to the comprehension of many different types of passages. This usually happens around the second and third grade, but even students still practicing decoding and very young pre-readers can learn to explore the **main idea** of a story and make predictions. Questions like "What was this book about?" and "What do you think character X will do next?" will help students make predictions and **summarize** or condense the main elements of a story.

As the stories read to students become more complex and as students begin reading their own stories, teachers can introduce other literary elements. Students of all ages generally enjoy stories with **themes**, or topics, that they can relate to or are already exploring. (Of course, *theme* can also mean the moral, lesson, or general statement about life a literary work conveys.) Integrated curricula, or those that structure several cross-curricular units around a central theme, are popular in many early childhood and some lower-elementary settings.

> ### Did You Know?
>
> The Supreme Court ruled in *Island Trees School District v. Pico* (1982) that a local school board may not remove books from junior high and high school libraries just because they dislike the ideas contained in them. However, controversy over student access to certain titles remains. Does your school or district have policies regarding the adoption of titles for the school library or classroom use?

Even without a formal daily or weekly theme in the classroom, teachers can help students make connections by integrating texts from other areas like science and social studies into literacy activities. For example, a unit on conservation might feature a story that includes a moral, or lesson, about the importance of conserving natural resources. Teachers might even encourage students to further explore their own interests and create their own integrated literary experiences by selecting and reading different works centered on a theme of their choosing.

Sample Question

15) John, a second-grade student, is assigned to read a paragraph from his social studies textbook and write a sentence stating the central idea. What can the reading teacher do to help him with this task if he gets stuck?
- A. ask him what he liked about what he read
- B. ask him to list all the details from the paragraph
- C. go over key vocabulary with him
- D. ask him what he thought was most important

Plot Diagrams

To facilitate deep comprehension of literary texts, teachers can help students understand key elements through a **plot diagram**. This graphic organizer helps students identify the **exposition**, or beginning, of the story, which sets the stage by describing the time, place, and main characters. Students can then pinpoint the **conflict** of the story, or the main struggle that drives the action. Next is the **rising action**, or sequence of events leading to the eventual climax, or turning point, which is the apex of the diagram.

> ### Check Your Understanding
>
> Practice filling out a plot diagram for a fiction text you are familiar with. Think about what texts you would recommend to teachers to introduce this concept.

The curve slopes sharply downward as the **falling action**, or results of the climax, unfolds. The diagram closes with the final resolution, or ending of the story. Depending on student age and grade level, teachers may introduce the idea that the resolution might not be happy, but all stories do have one.

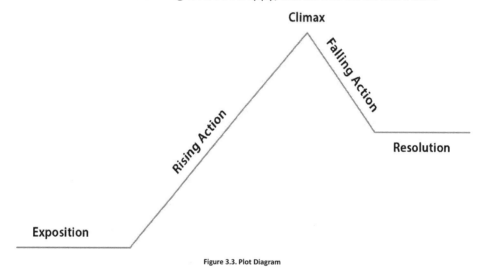

Figure 3.3. Plot Diagram

Introducing the plot diagram is easiest when students already have some background with a story. Teachers may draw on a popular children's movie or fairy tale to introduce these elements. Students struggling to comprehend a new text will have trouble understanding these elements. Timeless stories with plots that students know by heart are ideal for an initial exploration of the plot diagram.

Sample Question

16) A teacher wants to introduce her first-grade students to the idea of conflict in stories. Which technique is MOST appropriate?
   A. ask students to go to the library and select a storybook with lots of conflict
   B. project-based learning asking students to solve a major global problem
   C. have students compare and contrast problems in their lives they consider major and minor
   D. guided storybook reading in which the emphasis is on the problem the characters resolve

Nonfiction

Nonfiction is a genre of prose writing that is based in fact. Its information is, to the best of the author's knowledge, true and accurate. This does not mean, however, that nonfiction is dry or uninspiring.

Nonfiction writing comes in many forms, most of which display creativity and originality in how factual information is presented. **Literary nonfiction**, or **creative nonfiction**, for example, is a mix of expressive and informative writing that tells a true, verifiable, or documented story in a compelling, artistic way.

Author's Purpose

Nonfiction texts are written to persuade, inform, explain, entertain, or describe. Authors who write to **persuade** try to convince the reader to act or think a certain way. They may use specific reasons and supporting evidence to do this. Persuasive writers also use **rhetoric**, language chosen specifically for its particular effect, to influence readers.

Writing to **inform** is as straightforward as the term suggests: the author sets out simply to communicate information to the reader. Purely informative writing is found in many textbooks and news articles. Some informational writing may also **instruct** the reader. This type of writing includes items such as lists, steps to be followed, and a sequential order.

Similar to informing, some writing **explains**. It might explain how things are similar or different; it might define a term; it might explain a problem and its solution.

Nonfiction may also entertain. Typically, this type of writing will **narrate**, or tell a (true) story. Like fiction, narrative nonfiction (sometimes referred to as literary nonfiction) will include a setting, characters, and a plot. The writer may also use figurative language and other devices to entertain the reader.

Finally, nonfiction texts may **describe** something: a detailed description of an event, person, place, or even inanimate object.

The acronym **PIEED** helps students think about the author's purpose. It is accompanied by a picture of a pie with various slices to illustrate each of these purposes.

▶ **P**ersuade

▶ **I**nform

▶ **E**xplain

▶ **E**ntertain

▶ **D**escribe

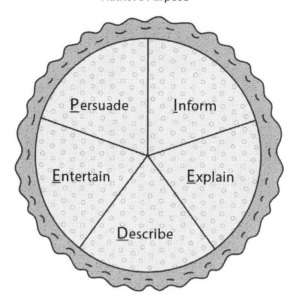

Figure 3.4. PIEED (Author's Purpose)

Nonfiction takes many forms, which are often related to the author's purpose:

▶ an essay is a short work about a particular topic or idea

▶ a speech is a short work with a specific purpose, intended to be presented orally in front of an audience

▶ a news article is a short recounting of a particular story

▶ a biography is a detailed, creative textual representation of a person's life

▶ an autobiography is an account of an individual's life, told by the individual

The author's purpose is sometimes further revealed by the text structure. For example, a problem-solution text structure is most likely to be used in a persuasive text. A compare and contrast structure is used to describe two like or unlike things. Transitional expressions that are part of the organizational pattern of the text can be used as clues for overall comprehension and in determining the author's purpose. Phrases like "most importantly" and "in contrast" are hints to the author's goal in writing.

Many educators use this step-by-step process to identify the purpose of a text.

1.   While reading the text, think of the question "Why did the author write this?"

2.   After reading, complete the statement "The author wrote this mainly to _____."

3.   Find important details in the text that support the statement. If no such details exist, the purpose statement might need to be modified.

Sample Question

17) An elementary teacher is working with students to identify the purpose of a science article. Which advice should the teacher give students to help them answer the question "What is the author's purpose?"?
   A. Always ask whether the author achieved their purpose for writing the text.
   B. Look for specific text evidence that supports a statement about the author's purpose.
   C. The purpose will generally be revealed explicitly in the introductory paragraph.
   D. A "call to action" never gives possible clues to the author's purpose.

Text Structure

Authors organize nonfiction texts with a text structure that suits their purpose. This structure may be a **sequence** of events, such as a news story about the days leading up to an important event. It might also be a thorough **description** of something, as in the opening paragraph of an essay describing a person or place in detail.

Many historical texts use a **cause-and-effect** pattern in which the cause is presented first, and the result is discussed next. A chapter in a social studies text about the Industrial Revolution, for example, might follow this pattern, citing the Industrial Revolution as the cause for a change in working and living conditions in many cities.

Other works are organized in a **problem-solution** structure, in which a problem is presented and then a possible solution discussed. Teachers might introduce this structure through a collaborative activity in which students identify a problem in the classroom, school, or community. They can then write a letter to a decision-maker about the issue and a possible solution. Finally, students can read other problem-solution texts to see how other authors structure their arguments.

Students can use a **compare and contrast** structure to explain how two things from their everyday experience are similar and different. Charts and other graphic organizers can help them organize their thoughts and understand this structure. A teacher might ask students, for example, to use a **Venn diagram** to determine the similarities and differences presented in a text.

It is helpful to integrate reading and writing nonfiction/expository texts that use the same text structure. This approach is used in many textbooks and curricular resources based on the Common Core State Standards.

Sample Question

18) A reading teacher is working with an interdepartmental team plan a cross-curricular lesson for a third grade social studies and ELA unit. One of the objectives is based on the following standards:

RI.3.8. Describe the logical connection between particular sentences and paragraphs in a text (e.g., comparison, cause/effect, first/second/third in a sequence). Which activity is MOST appropriate?
   A. Students read a historical narrative and then compare it to an argumentative essay.
   B. Students read a historical narrative and use a graphic organizer to map out causes and effects.
   C. Students read a historical narrative and underline the topic sentence of each paragraph.
   D. Students read a historical narrative and then write a personal narrative that includes sequencing

Identifying Central Ideas

Nonfiction texts contain a central or main idea. Identifying this idea is an important though sometimes challenging skill for students. This step is part of a process in which students master simpler skills before moving on to more advanced ones.

1. Students practice identifying the **topic** of the text. For example, the topic of a text might be "horses."

2. Students ask themselves a question such as "What is the author saying about horses?"

3. The answer to that question is the central idea of the text. "Horses are animals that have helped humans throughout history."

When using this method, students should not confuse topic with main idea. They should use the identification of the topic to determine the main or central idea.

The main idea of the text is stated explicitly or implicitly. When stated explicitly, the main idea is referred to as a **thesis** or thesis statement. Students can practice identifying the thesis of a short text before studying text with an implicitly stated main idea.

An implicit main idea is more difficult to identify. Students must **synthesize** or put together information and details from many parts of the text. The following process can help students identify the main idea.

1. Identify the main idea of each paragraph first. It might be stated explicitly as a topic sentence, or it might be implicit. If the idea is implicit, students will need to summarize the paragraph in a single sentence in their own words.

2. After determining the main idea of each paragraph, students can think about what these main ideas have in common or make a "summary of summaries."

3. Students should check their main idea statements to make sure they have no specific details or examples and that they encapsulate only the most important points.

Because identification of the central idea and summarization are similar thought processes, these skills are often taught together. Teachers might also introduce the central idea as the most important idea within the summary.

Students can use text organization and text features like headings and bolded terms to help them distinguish between central ideas and supporting details. Finally, students should understand that identifying the main idea of the text overall (and often of each paragraph) is not a skill to be used in isolation. Rather, it is a critical part of actively reading any nonfiction text.

Sample Question

19) A reading teacher is working with a small group of third-grade students to identify the main idea. When asked, "What is the main idea of the article?" students say, "Jupiter." What question should the interventionist ask next to guide students to identify the main idea?
   A. "What did you already know about Jupiter before reading?"
   B. "What are some new things you learned about Jupiter after reading?"
   C. "What is the author trying to teach us about Jupiter?"
   D. "What did you think was most interesting about Jupiter?"

Nonfiction Texts Across the Curriculum

Students encounter nonfiction texts throughout their coursework, so the reading teacher's role is not limited to working with ELA curricular resources. Other best practices for reading nonfiction texts across the curriculum are listed below:

▶ **Leveled nonfiction texts** can be used in multiple settings. Content area teachers can use texts on the same topic divided by complexity. Sites like the Smithsonian's *TweenTribune* and *Newsela* offer a variety of science and social studies texts for readers of all levels.

▶ Persuasive or argumentative texts that cover both sides of an issue can be used across the content areas to spark discussion and encourage higher-level analysis. When using such texts for instruction, teachers should ask students to analyze the author's rhetoric and use of **hyperbole**, or exaggerated language. Students should also determine whether a piece of persuasive writing has used any **logical fallacies**—errors in reasoning that weaken the argument.

▶ Nonfiction texts that are highly descriptive or that seek to describe a real-life work of art in words can be used as a springboard for creative expression in an art, music, or theater class.

▶ Students should be given explicit instruction in reading their textbooks or other resources in each course. For example, a science teacher might say, "As you read, underline or highlight the main idea in each paragraph and circle any words you do not know." This type of direction encourages active reading and makes any reading assignment more meaningful.

▶ Nonfiction texts should be carefully selected based on readability and appropriateness as well as alignment to standards. Reading teachers might be asked to review resources and make curricular recommendations for resources across content areas.

Sample Question

20) A teacher in a general education classroom that includes English language learners is working on an integrated science and ELA unit that involves a text on volcanoes. How should the teacher proceed to scaffold learning for the ELL students?

A. use graphic aids like diagrams and images in the text as much as possible to promote understanding

B. assign each student a peer tutor to read the text aloud to ensure correct pronunciation

C. provide English language learners with an audio recording of the text to listen to multiple times

D. avoid using the text and focus instruction on lectures and note-taking to meet the needs of all learners

Nonfiction Instructional Strategies

Comprehension strategies for nonfiction texts are similar to those for fiction texts, though nonfiction texts might be less predictable in purpose and structure. In expository texts, the writer wants to teach something to the reader. That means that students are learning something new from a factual perspective while also analyzing rhetorical techniques. Many of the strategies previously mentioned for literary texts can also be used for nonfiction texts, but there are additional considerations.

Students will encounter nonfiction texts more often than fiction texts both across the curriculum and in their everyday lives. They should be given plenty of strategies for overall comprehension of nonfiction texts.

Tap into or activate background knowledge by helping students draw connections between what they already know:

▶ Use a **brainstorm web**. Write the subject of the text in the center and encourage students to fill in the rest of the web with information they already know about the topic.

▶ **ABC brainstorm** in small groups or as a class. Students write one word or phrase they already know about the topic for each letter of the alphabet.

▶ **Free brainstorm** by asking students to freely write down (or draw) what they already know about a topic.

Students might be unfamiliar with certain terms they need to know to fully understand a nonfiction text. Help them by introducing subject-specific or challenging vocabulary before and during the reading. Strategies to introduce vocabulary include:

▶ **Word Expert**: Break up new vocabulary words into mini-lists and have each student become the "expert" of two or three words. Have students create a card with a definition, illustration, and sentence from the text to share with the class.

▶ **Words Alive**: Have students form groups to come up with actions or poses that illustrate the meaning of each new word on their list after the teacher explains the words' meanings to the group.

> **Study Tip**
>
> When you finish each chapter of this text, write down two or three terms that were new and/or that you believe you will have the most trouble remembering. Use a semantic map or the Frayer Model to help you remember each new term.

▶ **Semantic mapping**: Students write the new word in the center and then around it write a synonym, an antonym, an example, and a non-example of the word. Another take on this is the Frayer Model in which students write the word in the middle of four squares: definition, characteristics, examples, and non-examples.

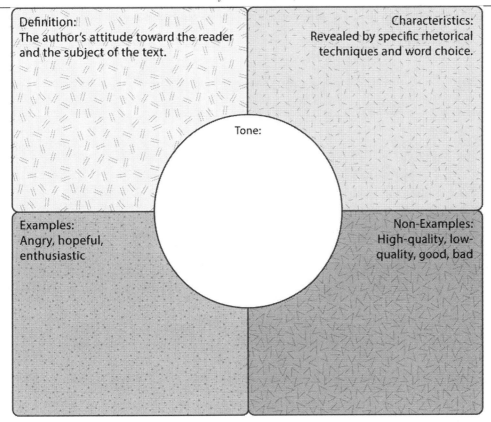

Figure 3.5. Frayer Model

Use collaborative learning strategies to tackle challenging nonfiction texts. Students can be divided into pairs for reading activities. They can also be placed in larger groups where each member works on a different part of the text (e.g., one student identifies the main idea of each paragraph, one student identifies the purpose).

Students should be taught and encouraged to use various annotation strategies. They should be encouraged to mark up the text, write in the margins, or use sticky notes. Using **text coding** can help students develop metacognition skills:

= I already know this

X = not what I expected

* = important

? = question about this

?? = really confused by this

! = surprising

L = learned something new

RR = section needs to be reread

In addition to annotating, students can use systematic **note-taking strategies**:

▶ Have students complete a full or partial outline of the text from a template.

▶ Have students use two-column notes where they put main ideas on one side and important details on the other. This is known as the **split-page method** or the **two-column method**.

▶ Have students use the **Cornell method** of note-taking whereby each page is divided into keywords, notes, and summary.

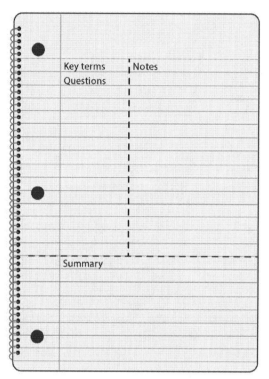

Figure 3.6. Cornell Method for Taking Notes

Finally, give students a toolbox of fix-up strategies for when comprehension breaks down. These might be similar to strategies used for fiction texts. For example:

▶ Students should know when and how to use the glossary in each textbook.

▶ Students should have access to a dictionary appropriate for their age and skill level to consult as needed.

▶ Students should know who to go to and how to ask for assistance when they have exhausted all their independent strategies.

Sample Question

21) Which strategy would first grade students be most likely to be successful in using?
    A. Cornell method
    B. Words Alive
    C. two-column method
    D. text coding

ANSWER KEY

1) **B.** Questioning a guest speaker would allow students to apply the listening skills they have learned in an authentic context.

2) **C.** In a class-wide debate, students have to think about the play critically, form an opinion, and then express that opinion orally.

3) **D.** The K stands for "What I already know" about the topic. The W is "What I want to know," and the L is completed after reading to state, "What I learned."

4) **B.** Fix-up strategies are applied when comprehension breaks down.

5) **C.** Students who are rewarded might read independently more and then discover they enjoy it.

6) **C.** This activity would allow for differentiation of text complexity.

7) **B.** Lexile measures only account for quantitative text features like word length and sentence length. They do not measure content, knowledge demands, and so on.

8) **D.** PALS partner students with a more proficient peer who provides scaffolding to help finish assignments.

9) **C.** Previewing the booklet's title and illustrations and making predictions about the book will help the student determine the genre of the book.

10) **B.** Drama is particularly useful for reader's theater, in which students read parts of a text aloud and develop oral reading skills and prosody.

11) **B.** An audio recording would help students challenged by reading written text understand the concepts of rhyme and meter.

12) **C.** This will model for students the thought process behind inferencing, such as finding relevant text evidence that supports an inference about a character.

13) **D.** Identifying specific evocative words will aid students in connecting word choice and tone.

14) **C.** Letters are usually written in the second person, so a teacher who wants students to avoid writing in the second person would probably not assign this project.

15) **D.** Asking John what he thought was most important about the text is a simple question that can help him think about the main or central idea.

16) **D.** Guided storybook reading emphasizing the problem the characters resolve is developmentally appropriate and a good introduction to the idea of conflict in literature.

17) **B.** Supporting text evidence is key to confirming answers on such a test and in confirming the author's purpose.

18) **B.** This activity integrates the two content areas and meets the objective by helping students identify cause/effect relationships in the text.

19) **C.** This question can help students narrow a topic to the main idea.

20) **A.** Graphic text features will help all learners, including English language learners, to understand key concepts visually, even if they lack the vocabulary skills to read the textbook chapter.

21) **B.** Even first-grade students can "act out" the meaning of new words and would likely find a Words Alive activity engaging.

4. Written Expression

Writing Skills and Reading Development

From a very young age, children understand that written language is a way to communicate. As they develop reading and writing skills, children learn that writing is a means to both express and receive information. When they produce writing, they are giving a reading experience to others. When they consume writing, they are engaged in their own reading experience. Both reading and writing help students develop pre-reading skills like letter-sound correspondence and phonemic awareness. For example, a student who titles a drawing "M" to denote it as an image of their mother understands that the symbol "M" stands for the sound /m/ and is part of communicating the meaning of "mother."

As students grow and develop more advanced literacy skills, writing-related activities like spelling practice can increase reading comprehension. Students who are exposed to high-frequency words in spelling or writing practice activities will strengthen their knowledge of these words. Since word identification skills are strongly linked to reading fluency, writing activities should be integrated with reading instruction and activities as much as possible.

Some theorists believe reading and writing are so interconnected that one cannot occur without the other. Even when students lack the motor skills to write themselves, many educators believe that writing can and should still be a meaningful part of literacy instruction.

Sample Question

1) Preschool children should be encouraged to experiment with letters and text to label pictures they draw because this
   A. strengthens receptive vocabulary.
   B. develops gross motor skills.
   C. contributes to an understanding of text as meaning.
   D. encourages the transition from artistic to written expression.

Developmental Stages of Writing

A child's journey to writing happens in phases and is influenced by encouragement from parents, teachers, and caretakers. **Writing development** involves three areas:

1. conceptual knowledge (understanding the purpose of writing)

2. procedural knowledge (understanding how to form letters and words)

3. generative knowledge (using words to communicate a meaning)

Even children as young as two begin to draw pictures they use to communicate ideas. These images are their first written representations. This drawing develops into **scribbling**, which looks like letters. Wavy scribbling or mock handwriting may appear as children are exposed to print-rich home environments and classrooms. This is followed by forms that look like individual letters and then forms with actual letters that resemble individual words strung together.

In the **transitional writing stage**, children begin writing letters separated by spaces, although real words are generally not yet being formed. Even in the transitional writing stage, however, many children successfully copy letters and words from environmental sources. Writing a child's name or the name of a common classroom object on a card for a child to copy can encourage transitional writing. Be mindful, however, that writing is still emergent, and children may invert letters or fail to accurately copy letters.

Table 4.1. Stages of Emergent Writing	
Stage	Example
Drawing	
Scribbling	
Wavy scribbles	
Letter-like forms	
Letter strings	

Table 4.1. Stages of Emergent Writing

Stage	Example
Transitional writing	stiM oiL
Invented and phonetic spelling	My NAM IS HANA
Word and phrase writing	DOG PiG
Conventional spelling and sentences	HANNAh

As children learn sounds, they begin a phase of **invented spelling**. They start communicating words and ideas more clearly, though many words may have only a beginning and ending sound. This stage is a natural part of the process of emergent writing. Children should be allowed to express ideas and practice writing without an overemphasis on spelling errors. Explicit spelling instruction will generally begin in the early elementary grades. Students will have plenty of time and practice to master these skills when they are developmentally ready.

As children gain more knowledge of sounds and words, they will begin writing whole words, first with single letter-sound constructions like "dog," "hat," and "fun." This progresses to the correct spelling of more words and eventually to stringing together words to make phrases and short sentences.

It is important to see writing as a process and recognize that it can be affected by many factors. For example, students with conditions that impact fine motor skills functioning or young children with developmental delays in associated domains may have difficulty learning to write fluently. Expectations should be tailored to the individual student. Teachers should encourage and praise effort rather than result as young people are developing these skills.

Table 4.2. Developmental Stages of Writing		
Stage	**Age**	**Students in this stage...**
Preconventional	3 – 5	▶ are aware that print conveys meaning, but they rely on pictures to communicate visually. ▶ include recognizable shapes and letters on drawings. ▶ can describe the significance of the objects in their drawings.
Emerging	4 – 6	▶ use pictures when drawing but may also label objects. ▶ can match some letters to sounds. ▶ copy print they see in their environment.
Developing	5 – 7	▶ write sentences and no longer rely mainly on pictures. ▶ attempt to use punctuation and capitalization. ▶ spell words based on sound.
Beginning	6 – 8	▶ write several related sentences on a topic. ▶ use word spacing, punctuation, and capitalization correctly. ▶ create writing that others can read.
Expanding	7 – 9	▶ organize sentences logically and use more complex sentence structures. ▶ spell high-frequency words correctly. ▶ respond to guidance and criticism from others.

Table 4.2. Developmental Stages of Writing		
Stage	**Age**	**Students in this stage...**
Bridging	8 – 10	▸ write about a particular topic with a clear beginning, middle, and end. ▸ begin to use paragraphs. ▸ consult outside resources (e.g., dictionaries).
Fluent	9 – 11	▸ write both fiction and nonfiction with guidance. ▸ experiment with sentence length and complexity. ▸ edit for punctuation, spelling, and grammar.

Sample Question

2) During free-choice center time, a kindergarten teacher notices that one of her students has gone to the writing center, taken a piece of lined paper, and written several misspelled phrases. What should the teacher do?

A. explain the correct spelling of each word
B. praise the student for the attempt and choosing to practice writing
C. provide hand-over-hand guidance for the student to erase and rewrite the words
D. target the student for more explicit spelling instruction

Foundations of Effective Writing

There are two primary theories on the act of writing. These are **the Simple View of Writing** and the **Not So Simple View of Writing**.

The Simple View of Writing maintains that there are two main parts of writing: transcription and ideation. Transcription refers to the physical act of writing and includes handwriting or typing skills and spelling skills. Ideation refers to the ability to think of and organize ideas. Ideation includes: idea generation, word choice, content, text, structure, and genre.

In graphic form, the simple view of writing is most often shown as:

$$IDEAS + TRANSCRIPTION = WRITING$$

The Not So Simple View of Writing adds another element: executive functioning (planning, reviewing and managing the writing).

In graphic form, the not so simple view of writing is most often shown as:

$$IDEAS + TRANSCRIPTION + EXECUTIVE\ FUNCTIONING = WRITING$$

It is important to understand that writing is a complex process, and thus for students to become effective writers, they must master many prerequisite skills. It is also important to identify what is meant by "effective" writing.

Effective writing has a central **focus**, or main idea (often referred to as a **central idea** in state and national standards). Brainstorming and other pre-writing activities can help students maintain focus as they plan a piece. While students will mainly be exposed to professional writing that has already been edited, having them identify the author's focus across a broad range of texts will increase reading and writing capability.

Additionally, students should identify how the author uses details, examples, and other elements as part of overall concept development. They should be critical of how authors support their arguments and determine whether the evidence is sufficient. Students can then use these skills to critically reflect on their own writing and decide whether they have adequately proven a point.

> **Did You Know?**
>
> Effective writing skills are a key component of success in higher education. Students who must take remedial or developmental college courses in writing and/or math (estimated at 40 – 60 percent) are less likely to complete their degree program on time or at all.

A knowledge of basic text **organization** will also help students become critical readers and effective writers. While there are many ways to organize and structure text, most effective writing has an **introduction**, several supporting details organized in a logical sequence, and a **conclusion** that wraps up the focus of the piece. It is helpful to have students practice labeling these parts in various texts. But even very young children can understand the idea of text organization by being shown the beginning, middle, and end of a story. As students edit and revise their work, they should organize their ideas so that the reader can follow the information in a logical pattern.

Each piece of writing also has a unique **style**, or approach. Style can describe the author's choice of words. Style also includes sentence and paragraph structure. Both word choice and structure can make a piece **formal**, **informal**, or somewhere in between. Additionally, all texts have a **tone** or attitude the author takes toward the subject or audience. A writer's tone might be hopeful, sarcastic, pessimistic, and so on.

One part of selecting a style and tone is the intended purpose and audience. Students should pay attention to the reader of their piece. A formal style is appropriate for writing a letter to the principal asking for a longer recess. A note to a friend would probably be written in an informal style. When reading any text, students should consider why an author chose a particular style convention or tone: Did the writer intend to argue a point to a hostile audience? Inform a group of students about the difference between income and expenses? Was the style formal or informal?

Mechanics are the structural elements of writing and include punctuation, capitalization, spelling, grammar, and general conventions of usage. Like most procedural knowledge of writing, this proficiency may vary among students and grade levels. A kindergarten class, for example, may be focused on a unit about capitalizing the letter *I*, whereas a second-grade class may be working on forming the past tense of verbs.

Teachers should not presume knowledge of Standard English conventions among students whose first language is not English. Correct use of prepositions, irregular verbs, and pronouns may be particularly challenging for these students until they get more experience with common usage patterns. Teachers should always aim for growth, not perfection, when helping students develop skills in editing their writing for errors in mechanics. These skills continue to build throughout a student's schooling.

Sample Question

3) A teacher is developing a rubric that she will use to score student writing. Which of the following categories would appear on the rubric under the heading of "mechanics"?
   A. word choice
   B. style
   C. punctuation
   D. tone

The Recursive Writing Process

Students should understand that writing is a process and that even professional writers put their work through several phases before releasing the finished product. A **recursive writing process** means that writers undertake various steps but may return to a previously completed part of the process. Also known as the **authoring cycle**, this process includes several phases in which ideas are transformed into written form to effectively communicate meaning:

1. Plan

2. Draft

3. Revise

4. Edit

5. Publish

The first step in planning is to **brainstorm** ideas, which can take many forms. Teachers might have the class generate ideas for topics and write them on the board or screen. Students can then create their own **webs** or **outlines** to organize their ideas.

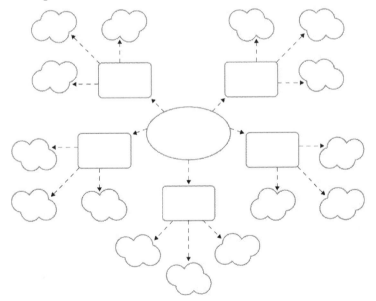

Figure 4.1. Brainstorming Web

Study Tips

Freewriting, questioning, listing, clustering/webbing, and outlining are some of the most common pre-writing or planning activities. Make a chart of each and then list which age groups and types of writing assignments you would recommend each planning activity for.

This initial planning can help students organize their overall point and supporting details. These activities can be based on a book they have read, their opinion of the work (e.g., "I liked the book," "I did not like the book," "My favorite/least favorite part was...") and reasons for their opinion. Students might also write a simple expository piece introducing a topic and then using supporting details to inform the reader. Brainstorming activities can also help students organize the events they want to describe when writing narratives.

After brainstorming, students **draft** their piece and connect their ideas with an introductory statement, support, and concluding section. With scaffolding, students then go through a **revision** process where they address weaknesses in the writing. For example, they may need to add more supporting details or connecting words ("because," "also," "then") to improve clarity. They can then **edit** for capitalization, end marks, and spelling. Teachers can help students in the revision process by giving them a simple checklist to help ensure they have met certain criteria. One such checklist is the **COPS mnemonic**, which stands for Capitalization, Organization, Punctuation, and Spelling.

Teachers can also use peer and teacher feedback as part of the revision process. Receiving feedback helps students understand that the main purpose of writing is to communicate ideas, so having other readers offer their perceptions and suggestions is an important part of revision.

Students should **publish** their work after the final copy is created, particularly if the writing project was significant in scope. Having students read their work aloud is one simple and immediate way to publish a piece (as well as a way to link reading and writing), as is posting it on a classroom or school bulletin board. Teachers may have students organize and bind their work into a simple book with string or brads or collect student work into a class-wide literary sampler.

If a teacher uses student portfolios in the classroom, students can prepare their pieces for inclusion in a digital or physical folder. This may involve transcribing the piece digitally, adding illustrations, or matting it on construction paper. Teachers should also emphasize that sharing the work with others is an important part of publishing. This is a great way to build a home–school connection while encouraging students to share their work with parents. Teachers should also show student work samples or portfolios at parent conferences to further build the home–school connection.

Sample Question

4) An upper elementary teacher sponsors a creative writing club that meets weekly after school. What is a high-impact way to publish student work from the club and share it with the school community?
   A.   invite administrators to attend one of the club meetings and listen to students read their work
   B.   encourage students to read their pieces at home to their family members
   C.   plan a digital or print literary journal that can be shared across the school
   D.   teach students to use publishing and graphic design software to format their pieces

Instructional Strategies for Developing Writing Skills

Teachers can use many strategies and activities to help students develop strong writing skills throughout the writing process.

Planning

1. **Data dump** is an informal prewriting method whereby students write down a topic and then any words that immediately come to mind. For example, a student might write "environmentalism" and then list terms like "climate change, pollution, endangered animals, etc." After a data dump, students select only the words that most closely pertain to their chosen topic.

2. In **guided pre-writing**, the class or group of students come up with ideas and/or a writing structure. The teacher helps by visually projecting ideas or writing them on a board. Mapping, outlining, webbing, and listing are common strategies for guided pre-writing.

3. **RAFT** is a prewriting method that encourages students to consider their purpose, audience, and organization pattern. Students think about the following questions:

Role of writer: what perspective will you as the writer take?

Audience: who will read the piece?

Format: how will you communicate your message (e.g., story, essay, drama)?

Topic: what will you write about?

4. **Media or tech-enabled planning** involves students watching a video, looking at images, or searching for ideas online. This can be a useful strategy for students who are stuck or who do not have an opinion on an issue or a clear topic to write about.

Drafting

1. **Framed paragraphs** are a scaffolding technique to help students write paragraphs. Framed paragraphs are fill-in-the-blank templates that students use to write their own paragraphs. For example, an "empty" frame for a persuasive paragraph might be something like:

I think that _____. The first reason I think this is because_____.
The second reason I think this is because_____. Lastly, I
believe that_____. For these
reasons_____should_____.

2. **Paragraph or essay hamburgers** encourage students to plan a paragraph or essay with the topic sentence or introduction as the top "bun" and the concluding sentence or concluding

paragraph as the bottom "bun." The supporting details or body paragraph are the middle parts of the "hamburger."

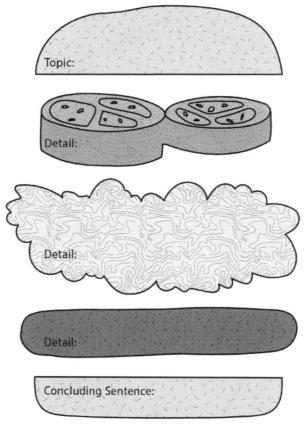

Figure 4.2. Paragraph Hamburger

3. Shared or interactive writing is a process whereby writers are scaffolded by "experts," usually teachers. In shared writing, the teacher scribes for the students, who must give explicit direction in what to write. This can be an effective method for students who have difficulty with the physical task of writing. In interactive writing, students compose the written piece, but the teacher serves as the subject matter expert who facilitates the process.

In both methods, the teacher helps scaffold learning as needed. This might involve asking leading questions ("What should happen after_____?"), providing ideas for transitions or breaks ("Let's start our next sentence with 'Additionally,'"), or even providing more explicit instruction to reinforce concepts ("Now, we need to add supporting details. What supporting details can we add?"). Shared or interactive writing helps students see and participate in an effective model for writing, which can give them confidence and strategies to use in independent writing assignments.

Revision and Editing

1. **Modeling or think-alouds** can be used with a sample piece. This can be teacher- or student-authored (with student permission and name removed as requested) but should involve whole-class input. The piece can be projected on a screen and edited through a "track changes" feature in a word-processing program or even copied onto a transparency and written on. This process is helpful, as it allows students to participate in and experience the revision and editing process. Teachers can encourage input from the

class and model strategies to revise writing, such as reading aloud, identifying and refining thesis and topic sentences, and so on.

2. **Conferencing or peer review** can also be used after first modeling the process and providing guidelines to students. Research proves that the most successful writing conferences are structured and occur when students have a clear idea of what type of feedback they should provide and how to give feedback in a constructive way.

3. **Self-assessment** should also be taught as part of the revision process. Students can be given a checklist or rubric from which to assess their own drafts and make necessary revisions.

Sample Question

5) A third-grade teacher wants to encourage students to organize their thoughts into a coherent paragraph. Which of the following instructional strategies BEST meets this goal?
   A. data dump
   B. self-assessment
   C. hamburger method
   D. COPS mnemonic

Spelling, Usage, and Mechanics

Spelling Instruction

The mechanics of writing will generally involve explicit **spelling** instruction, which will likely be part of a program's curriculum. Educators should note that spelling (as the process of encoding) and reading (as the process of decoding) are reciprocal skills and will have an impact on each other.

It is important to view spelling as part of a developmental continuum and not overemphasize correct spelling too early when preschool students are still forming mock letters or letter strings. However, a standard **continuum of spelling** can be referenced to tailor spelling instruction appropriate to grade level while always keeping in mind the differing developmental levels within the classroom.

Table 4.4 Continuum of Spelling	
By the end of firstwords with . . . correctly spell short should be able to grade, most students	high-frequency words (chat, that) [CCVC]consonant blends and digraphs in simple and simple consonant-vowel pattern (go, no) [CV]vowel-consonant pattern (up, egg) and [VC]sonant (cat, dog, pin) pattern [CVC]short vowel sounds with a consonant-verb-con
words with . . . should be spelling grade, most students By the end of second	final consonant blends (rant, fast, bend, link)r-controlled vowels (near, bear, hair, are)more complex long vowel patterns (suit, fail)double consonant endings (lick, fuss)regular long vowel patterns (ride, tube) [CVC][CVCC]
words with . . .should be able to spell grade, most students By the end of third	words with suffixes that show number or degree(fastest, foxes)compound wordstwo-syllable wordscontractionswhose)advanced digraphs and blends (phase, character, silent consonants (tomb, known, gnaw, wrote)short vowel patterns (head, sought)soft g's and c's (dice, hedge)contractionswhose)advanced digraphs and blends (phase, character, silent consonants (tomb, known, gnaw, wrote)short vowel patterns (head, sought)soft g's and c's (dice, hedge)diphthongs (coil, soon, enjoy, wow)
words with . . .should be able to spell grade, most students By the end of third	special spelling rules such as doubling the final letter of CVC words when adding certain suffiexes(napping, saddest)

Spelling instruction should be explicit and systematic. Such instruction is part of what is known as **structured literacy**, an approach where all components of literacy are taught systematically and explicitly.

Spelling instruction focuses on **orthographic knowledge**, or an understanding of the system by which spoken language is communicated in writing. To develop orthographic knowledge, students must have certain foundational skills based on an understanding of the three layers of linguistic information:

▶ alphabetic: recognition of letter-sound correspondence and sounding out from left to right

▶ pattern: understanding more complex patterns that might not be simple left to right, such as long vowel digraphs or open and closed syllables

▶ meaning: understanding meaning in word parts that do not change with pronunciation, such as "sign" and "signature"

To spell, students need skills in visualization and auditory sequencing. **Visualization** is the ability to recall the spelling of a word and write it based on a stored mental image. **Auditory sequencing** is the ability to identify a word's sounds in the proper order. These skills are linked to both reading and spelling proficiency and are important foundations.

Spelling instruction should focus on instruction and assessment. Examples of research-backed spelling instructional activities include:

▶ Word sorts: students sort words based on orthographic features. For example, students might sort words with long and short vowel sounds or words that end in *–ch*.

▶ Phonogram study: students practice reading and writing words that contain certain sounds, like /ou/, or word endings, like *–ink*.

▶ Writing sorts: students divide spelling words into columns based on similar orthographic patterns.

▶ Spelling notebooks: students learn a spelling rule (or exception to it) and then list words that demonstrate it.

▶ Cover-copy-compare: students study word spellings, cover them up, and then spell them independently, checking afterward for accuracy.

Like other elements of literacy instruction, a multisensory approach is also useful, especially for students with learning differences. Some multi-sensory approaches include:

➢ Finger spelling, where student segment the word with fingers and/or write the letters of the word on palms as they spell it

➢ Practice spelling words in sand, shaving cream, or mud

➢ Using magnetic letters or letter tiles to practice spelling words

➢ Changing the tone of voice while spelling words orally (e.g. louder voice for vowels and softer voice for consonants)

➢ Hopping or jumping rope while spelling words orally

It is also important to provide opportunities for students to apply spelling skills in writing. Students can write a paragraph or essay using words from a spelling list or words with a certain orthographic pattern. Students must be explicitly taught that the purpose of studying spelling is to become a competent writer, not a perfect speller. Students must receive many opportunities to *apply* spelling skills as part of the drafting and revision process.

Regardless of specific activities and approaches, educators should assess spelling proficiency in multiple contexts. This means that assessment of student progress should not rely solely on traditional spelling tests. It should include authentic assessments, both formal and informal, as educators monitor students' overall writing development.

Sample Question

6) A fourth grader writes the following sentence:

I should have called him, but he wuld not have been home.

What type of spelling instruction should his teacher use to help him revise this sentence?
- A. draw his attention to the correctly spelled phonogram in the sentence
- B. point out the incorrectly spelled word and have him write the word spelled correctly five times
- C. have him read aloud the sentence he has written to identify and correct his spelling error
- D. use an incidental approach and try to develop opportunities for him to see the word spelled correctly in another text

Mechanics Instruction

Mechanics instruction used to focus on drills, and many students did not understand the connection between explicit study of grammatical conventions and their own writing. In recent years, however, most classrooms use a more integrated or holistic approach where mechanics and writing are taught together.

Many teachers and contemporary educational publishers focus on how a certain grammatical convention conveys a message in a particular way, instead of focusing on structure of language in isolation, which is not as helpful and may hinder oral and written language development. For example, capitalization and punctuation may not be necessary or appropriate when texting. However, in a formal expository essay for an academic audience, attention to these details is essential.

Further, correct punctuation such as commas and semicolons help readers follow a writer's message and clearly see the relationship between ideas. For instance, short, choppy sentences structured in a nearly identical way may not appeal to or interest certain audiences.

Some best practices and instructional techniques for teaching mechanics in context are discussed below.

1. **Writing workshop** is an organizational framework for teaching the writing process that includes a mini-lesson, work time, and share time. The mini-lesson can provide mechanics instruction for students to incorporate into their writing.

2. **Targeted mechanics instruction** can be used with an individual student or at the class level. For example, after grading a student-authored short story, a teacher may need to provide explicit instruction in apostrophe use as a targeted lesson to the entire class. Or perhaps a teacher notices that only one or two students are struggling with correct use of apostrophes. The teacher could then provide individualized instruction, perhaps through published exercises in a text or on a digital platform.

3. Teachers can use **mentor texts** to teach grammar. Mentor texts describe high-quality writing (often published) that students can emulate in their own writing. These types of texts can be used to teach punctuation, capitalization, dialogue, sentence structure, style, format, and appropriateness to audience.

4. Teachers can give students **writing assignments** to practice and demonstrate understanding of key components of mechanics. For example, students can write a paragraph with two compound sentences and two complex sentences or an essay in which they identify and circle all the object or subject pronouns they used.

5. Teachers can encourage reading and **analysis** of structure. After reading texts, students can consider how the texts use conventions to create meaning and engage the reader. Possible questions for analysis include:

▸ How are pronouns used to create perspective?

▸ How is sentence structure used to create tone and mood?

▸ How are sentences and dialogue punctuated? How does this help the reader?

▸ How might the meaning of the text have shifted if different choices in mechanics had been used?

6. Teachers can encourage varied **writing exercises** for different purposes and encourage writing every day. Not all writing exercises have to be formal or instructional. Educators should allow time for freewriting as well as for writing that will be graded in part based on use of mechanics appropriate to the audience and situation.

7. Teachers should be mindful and respectful of dialects and registers. **Dialect** is an overall characteristic of a group of speakers. For example, certain English speakers are said to speak in a dialect based on geographic location (e.g., a Southern drawl or a Boston accent). A **register** is a variation in language based on audience or situation. Students may slip into various dialects and even registers as they write. Educators should not be critical of such variations. Rather, they should encourage students to think about a given audience when they write and how they can most clearly communicate their message with that audience in mind.

Sample Question

7) A teacher is looking for mentor texts to use to provide instruction to students on punctuation of dialogue. What type of texts would be most appropriate?
   A.   autobiographies about well-known people
   B.   persuasive essays with expert quotations
   C.   long narrative poems with multiple speakers
   D.   short stories with multiple characters

Inquiry and Research

The Research Process

Research and library skills are an important part of developing overall student literacy. There are seven steps in the research process:

1. **Identifying and focusing on the topic**. This might be as simple as having students pick a topic they want to learn more about or develop a research question they wish to answer—before searching online.

2. **Finding background information and conducting a preliminary search.** This involves getting a general overview of a topic and possible subtopics. During this stage students may Google a topic or read the Wikipedia page about a particular topic.

3. **Locating materials.** This could involve work at the library and online. Teachers should encourage students to explore a wide variety of possible resources. Depending on the research topic, students should seek out **primary sources**, or firsthand accounts. Primary sources may be speeches or diaries, surveys or census data, photographs of an event, and several other media that give eyewitness accounts of an event. Many primary sources are available online, and many sites organize these sources into an accessible format for students. Many materials that students find will also be **secondary sources**, or non-firsthand accounts. These include the majority of books, articles, and web pages devoted to a topic.

> **Did You Know?**
>
> Some state standards require students to know the differences between primary and secondary accounts, so this type of analysis should be part of the research process.

4. **Evaluating sources.** Students should determine if certain sources are useful and accessible to them. For example, a library database may generate results for articles in publications the library does not have. Some resources may be overly technical or written for an older audience. Students should also make sure they have **credible sources** written by experts. This stage in the research process might be a good point to introduce the different types of information available on the internet and the elements that make a source more reliable (listed author, .edu or .org domain, publication date, and so on).

5. **Note-taking.** Note-taking may involve the use of formal note cards or simply jotting down main ideas. As developmentally appropriate per student age, teachers should ensure students understand the idea of paraphrasing, or changing the author's words into their own, as they take notes. Paraphrasing can help students prevent **plagiarizing**, or presenting someone else's words as their own work.

6. **Writing.** This includes organizing all the notes into sentences and paragraphs. Students should be aware of the overall organization of their work as they introduce a focused topic, provide support, and write a conclusion. Depending on the age group teachers work with, they may have students make a poster to present their research instead of writing a formal paper.

7. **Citing sources.** This may include in-text **citations** and preparing a **bibliography**. To simplify these elements for young students, teachers might have them simply list titles of books and authors. Students in the upper elementary grades can create more sophisticated bibliographies in MLA style. MLA is generally regarded as the simplest citation style and the one students are first introduced to.

These steps can be simplified for very young students and depending on the scope of the research project. However, even kindergartners can gather information from sources to answer a simple research question, and first-grade students can contribute to a class-wide research project with teacher support. The key is introducing students to the various parts of the research process while providing scaffolding as needed to support them as they explore new outlets for their developing literacy.

Sample Question

8) Which of the following is a primary source appropriate for a third-grade class to use as part of a research project?

    A. an article in a history journal written by a noted scholar of WWII at a 770 Lexile level

    B. photographs of soldiers taken during WWII available online

    C. a documentary video about American pilots in WWII made by public television

    D. transcripts of an interview with a WWII pilot at a 1400 Lexile level

Digital Tools

Increasingly, schools are using digital learning tools in their curricula. Many schools have one or more subscriptions to various educational technology platforms that may enhance student learning and digital literacy, which is defined as the ability to find, use, and create digital information. **Media literacy**, a key part of digital literacy, is students' ability to access, analyze, evaluate, and communicate information in both digital and physical form.

Some students may be experienced with accessing digital information at home on computers, tablets, or phones. However, not all students will have the same level of **digital literacy**. Teachers should explicitly direct students in strategies for finding and assessing the usefulness of digital information. The internet has created an unlimited platform for disseminating information. Students must be taught early not to trust all sources equally and how to determine the validity and usefulness of a given source.

> ### Did You Know?
>
> There are many intentionally fake sites on the internet designed to help students practice determining whether online information is legitimate. One example is found at https://zapatopi.net/treeoctopus, where students can learn about the Pacific Northwest Tree Octopus.

Digital tools also enable students to differentiate literacy instruction through adaptive software programs that target practice for individual skill level. Technological tools can also aid students with special needs or limited English proficiency through their daily activities in the classroom. Devices and applications that allow nonverbal children to communicate and those that help English language learners quickly translate new words may become indispensable learning aids.

Teachers should also incorporate digital tools into the writing process as appropriate. Suggestions include:

▶ Having students watch videos or go online to gather ideas during the prewriting process

▶ Having students create digital webs or outlines during the prewriting process

▶ Having students draft their work in a in a shared online document that other students and the teacher can access to give feedback

▶ Having students post drafts to a class portal or drive to give and receive feedback

▶ Using a digital class discussion board to share ideas and best practices or simply to practice writing and responding to others

▶ Publishing student work on appropriate digital pages such as a school website or through a reputable organization that publishes student writing

▶ Encouraging students to add multimedia elements to their writing

Sample Question

9) What is the best argument in favor of technology in the reading classroom?
   A. Students use technology at home, so they should also use it at school.
   B. Technology may help differentiate instruction for struggling readers.
   C. Many texts are available for free online.
   D. Technology is not bad as long as it is strictly controlled by the teacher.

ANSWER KEY

1) **C.** This activity helps young children understand that written language is used to communicate meaning.

2) **B.** Practice is essential to developing writing and spelling skills, so praise is appropriate because the student chose this activity. Further, the student is likely in the normal and necessary invented spelling stage.

3) **C.** Punctuation is a major part of the mechanics of writing.

4) **C.** A school-wide literary journal is an effective way to publish and distribute creative writing in a high school.

5) **C.** The hamburger method helps students understand what sentences go where in a paragraph and how they can structure a paragraph to communicate a point.

6) **A.** This is an evidence-based spelling strategy. The student can be prompted to recognize that "should" and "would" have similar orthographic patterns and should be spelled similarly.

7) **D.** Students can see a model of dialogue punctuated correctly and then structure their own work in a similar way.

8) **B.** This is a primary source that is easily accessible to third-grade students.

9) **B.** This is one benefit that may help his students and that he might have a hard time arguing against.

5. Meeting the Needs of Diverse Learners

English Language Learners

Second-Language Acquisition

Researchers agree that **second-language acquisition** occurs, much like first-language acquisition, through a series of stages. Learners must pass through each of the five stages on their way to proficiency, though the time spent in each stage varies from person to person.

The first stage—**preproduction**—is also known as the **silent period**. Though these learners may have upward of 500 words in their receptive vocabulary, they refrain from speaking. However, they will listen and may copy words down. They can respond to visual cues such as pictures and gestures, and they will communicate their comprehension.

Sometimes students will repeat what they hear in a process called parroting. This can help them build their receptive vocabulary, but it should not be mistaken for producing language.

In the **early production** stage, learners achieve a 1,000-word receptive and active vocabulary. They can now produce single-word and two- to three-word phrases and can respond to questions and statements as such. Many learners in this stage enjoy musical games or word plays that help them memorize language chunks (groups of related words and phrases) they can use later.

English language learners have a vocabulary of about 3,000 words by the time they reach the **speech emergence stage** of second-language acquisition. They are able to chunk simple words and phrases into sentences that may or may not be grammatically correct. They respond to models of proper usage better than they do to explicit correction.

At this stage, learners are more likely to have conversations with native English speakers, as they are gaining confidence in their language skills. These students can understand simple readings when reinforced by graphics or pictures and can complete some content work with support.

Did You Know?

Morpheme acquisition order is the pattern in which the knowledge of morphemes is gained as people acquire language. Within first-language acquisition, the pattern remains consistently fixed for most learners. For English language learners, the pattern is less constant and varies based on first language.

By the **intermediate fluency stage**, English language learners have a vocabulary of about 6,000 words. They can speak in more complex sentences and catch and correct many of their errors. They are also willing to ask questions to clarify what they do not understand. Learners at this stage may communicate fairly well, but they have large gaps in their vocabulary and in their grammatical and syntactical understanding of the language. They are often comfortable with group conversations as long as any difficult academic vocabulary is limited.

Second-language learners reach **advanced fluency** when they have achieved cognitive language proficiency in their

learned language. They demonstrate near-native ability and use complex, multi-phrase and multi-clause sentences to convey their ideas. Though learners at this stage still have accents and sometimes use idiomatic expressions incorrectly, they are essentially fluent.

As language learners progress through levels of study, they usually develop an interlanguage to aid them in their progression. **Interlanguage** is the learner's current understanding of the language they are learning. It is a rule-based system that develops over time. It tends to blend aspects of the learner's first language with those of the second.

Interlanguage is often characterized by the learner's tendency to overgeneralize speaking and writing rules in the new language. For example, when students learn that most English verbs in the past tense end in –*ed*, they might apply this rule to all verbs. The learner then creates an interlanguage rule by continuing to conjugate irregular verbs incorrectly. Over time, these rules are adjusted and readjusted according to feedback, and the interlanguage evolves as the learner moves toward proficiency.

When language learners stop progressing and the development of their interlanguage stops, their understanding can become fossilized. **Fossilization** is the point in second-language acquisition when a learner's growth freezes, and further linguistic development becomes highly unlikely.

Sample Question

1) Lucia enjoys listening to songs in English. She memorizes the choruses and sings them to herself. She notes words she does not recognize and integrates phrases from the songs into her everyday language practice. When asked about the songs, Lucia responds in single words and short phrases but struggles to compose complete sentences. What stage of second-language acquisition might Lucia be in?

- A. preproduction
- B. early production
- C. speech emergence
- D. intermediate fluency

First-Language and Second Language

First and second language acquisition are both similar and different.

Similarities	Differences
Both include a silent period	Explicit instruction is not always needed in L1
Both go through typical development stages	Typically many opportunities to practice with native speakers when learning L1
Both improve through exposure and practice	Grammatical rules of L1 are easier to learn through experience
Errors are usually a part of the learning process of both	More difficult to reach native-like fluency in L2
Understanding or comprehension happens before production (speaking)	L2 learning is a more active and conscious process

Additionally, students' first languages will always impact their learning of English. The influences will occur in all parts of language learning, from grammatical understanding to vocabulary acquisition to syntactical awareness. They are bound to transfer their understanding of their first language to their studies of English to make sense of what they are learning.

Transfer occurs when a student applies knowledge of a first language to another. Transfer can be both positive and negative. **Positive transfer** occurs when students find similarities between their native language and English and use those similarities to help them learn.

For example, a Spanish-speaking student may recognize the English verb "to comprehend" because it looks like the Spanish verb *comprender* ("to understand"). Visually similar words like these are **cognates**. Words that look similar but are different in meaning are **false cognates**. The Spanish verb *comprar*, for example, means "to buy," not "to compare." Students who are learning a new language should understand that both cognates and false cognates exist.

> **Did You Know?**
>
> Students' ability to recognize cognates and use them as a tool for understanding a second language is called **cognate awareness**.

Negative transfer, also called interference, occurs when students incorrectly apply rules from their native language to their learning of English. For example, a Spanish-speaking student may place an adjective after a noun ("the house red") because of the noun-adjective structure in Spanish. However, in English the adjective comes before the noun ("the red house").

Code-switching is also frequent among language learners. Students mix words from their first language in with the language they are learning. This happens when they have forgotten a term or do not know how to express themselves in the second language. For example, a Spanish-speaking student who is looking for the bathroom and cannot recall a vocabulary word might ask, "Where is the *baño*?" This type of linguistic back-and-forth is very common with bilingual and multilingual individuals.

Finally, students' **accents** will impact their learning and pronunciation of English. Often speakers will substitute the sounds of their first language for ones they think are the same in English. For example, some Spanish speakers may pronounce the /v/ sound like the English *b*.

Additionally, stresses and intonations of words can be carried from first languages. Both of these speech patterns can change the meanings of English words (for example, the meanings of the words "read" and "read"), leading to an unclear message.

Sample Question

2) Jamie speaks Spanish as his native language and has just moved to the United States from Mexico. He is enrolled in second-grade class where the other students speak English. A few weeks in, Jamie is still reluctant to speak because he mixes in words from his first language with the English he is learning. Which linguistic behavior is Jamie demonstrating?
   A. code-switching
   B. cognate awareness
   C. difficulty with accent
   D. language interference

Assessment of English Language Learners (ELLs)

Because English language learners need differentiated instruction, they should be identified as soon as possible. Title III of Part A of ESSA requires states to hold English language learners to the same rigorous standards as all students. These students must receive high-quality, early targeted interventions to increase English proficiency and stay on track to meet grade-level objectives.

The first and most common step in identifying English Language learners (ELLs) is the **home language survey**. Many states and districts mandate that parents complete this upon student enrollment. This survey is short (fewer than ten questions) and available in multiple languages. An example survey is shown below.

Student Name:	Grade:	Date:
Parent/Guardian Name: _____ Parent/Guardian Signature: _____		
Right to Translation and Interpretation Services	1. In what language(s) would your family prefer to communicate with the school? _____	
Eligibility for Language Development Support	2. What language did your child learn first? _____ 3. What language does your child use the most at home? _____ 4. What is the primary language used in the home, regardless of the language spoken by your child? _____ 5. Has your child received English language development support in a previous school? Yes___ No___ Don't Know___	
Prior Education	6. In what country was your child born? _____ 7. Has your child ever received formal education outside of the United States? (Kindergarten – 12th grade) ____Yes ____No If yes: Number of months: _____ Language of instruction: _____ 8. When did your child first attend a school in the United States? (Kindergarten – 12th grade) _____ Month Day Year	

Figure 5.1. Home Language Survey

The home language survey is not the end of the process. Some parents might fear that their child will be placed in "lower-level" classes, so they may say that English is spoken in home when it is not. In other cases, students who speak a language other than English at home may be fluent in both languages and require no language learning supports at school. However, in many states and districts, all students who

use a language other than English at home must receive further assessment to determine the need for English language learning services. Some commercially available assessment instruments include:

1. Bilingual Syntax Measure (BSM) of listening and speaking

2. IDEA Proficiency Test (IPT)

3. Language Assessment System (LAS Links)

4. WIDA-ACCESS Placement Test

5. Woodcock-Muñoz Language Survey–Revised (WMLS–R)

6. Student Oral Language Observation Matrix (SOLOM) (particularly useful if the second language is not Spanish)

Some states also use scores below a certain threshold on standardized achievement tests as possible indications of limited English proficiency, particularly for older students (grade 2 and above).

State requirements for qualifications to administer ELL assessments vary. In some locations, ESOL or bilingual education teachers might give such assessments. In others, reading teachers are responsible, particularly if they are proficient in the student's first language.

Reading teachers work closely with other teachers and administrators specially trained in second language acquisition to make sure the assessment process is thorough and expedient.

If a reading teacher conducting an assessment determines that the student needs to be tested for English proficiency, they should consult with the appropriate specialist to ensure the student is assessed by the most qualified individual.

The assessment is typically followed by an interview with the student's parents or guardians, with an interpreter as needed. This step is crucial, as it can give relevant background on the student's prior educational experiences and other factors that might not be apparent through the home language survey and the assessment.

In some states, particularly those with many English language learners, a **Language Proficiency Assessment Committee** (LPAC) may be formed. An LPAC is composed of relevant educators and administrators. This committee recommends placement of ELLs into certain courses and creates a plan for their success. (These committees are similar to an IEP but focus on language-learning goals.) Depending on the school's student population and resources, reading teachers may participate on such committees. However, they must be aware of student plans and monitor their implementation as part of students' overall literacy development.

Reading teachers must consider all aspects of a student's learning situation. Formal assessment measures like standardized tests and other high-stakes assessments may not fully reflect an ELL's abilities. Educators should use frequent, ongoing informal assessment measures to help confirm any placement decisions made through standardized assessments.

Students who require special education services or reading intervention services are in another category. Many schools and districts use a multidisciplinary approach to identify students for special services. This approach requires input from special education teachers, ESOL teachers, reading specialists, school psychologists, and others.

Students who are misplaced (e.g., a student is thought to have a second language acquisition issue when they actually have a learning disability) will not receive appropriate services and programming.

Further, it is not unusual that a student might need English language learning support *and* qualify for special education services. ESOL teachers may initiate referrals for special education services as appropriate. A student might need evaluation by multiple professionals before the best services to meet individual needs are found.

Sample Question

3) Which is the MOST appropriate question to ask parents or guardians during an interview as part of a comprehensive assessment of English language learning?

- A. "Do you value education in your home?"
- B. "Has your child attended school before?"
- C. "Why did you come to the United States?"
- D. "Why do you believe learning English is important?"

Instruction of English Language Learners

Like all learners, ELLs need developmentally appropriate systematic instruction to build content knowledge and English proficiency. While students are working to master content-specific standards, they will also be working to master **English Language Proficiency (ELP) standards**. Such standards may be created by the state or by the WIDA Consortium (a group of state and government agencies that uses a shared set of ELPs). These standards aim to help students develop language proficiencies related to language arts, mathematics, science, social studies, and the social and instructional language of the school environment.

> **Did You Know?**
>
> Some schools use bilingual education to transition to solely English instruction. Other schools use full English immersion with ESOL services, through co-teaching, pull-out services, or sheltered or specialized classes.

Within a broader framework of overarching ELPs, educators should create language objectives for ELLs that correspond with each lesson's focus. In schools with a large population of English language learners, some classes may be "sheltered." These classes focus on the content area and English language learning, with an emphasis on developing language objectives in conjunction with content area proficiency.

However, if ELL students are taught in the general education setting, content area teachers will need to embed English learning objectives in their lessons. They will also need to modify lessons and assessments to meet the needs of all learners. This might include strategies such as:

- ▶ using picture dictionaries or electronic translators
- ▶ eliminating portions of assignments or assessments students may not have background knowledge of
- ▶ using peer tutors or collaborative learning strategies that build on each student's strengths
- ▶ using multimedia or visual elements to aid in understanding
- ▶ pre-teaching core vocabulary or vocabulary scaffolding such as digital texts with click-through definitions
- ▶ limiting teacher talk and, when used, avoiding colloquialisms and speaking slowly
- ▶ verifying that instructions are understood before students begin a task

- ▶ providing both a print and oral version of instructions

- ▶ using manipulatives or authentic learning situations whenever possible

- ▶ providing copies of lecture notes or allowing audio recording

- ▶ When conducting assessments with English language learners, some common strategies include:

- ▶ giving students a word bank or other explicit prompting

- ▶ allowing a test to be read aloud or to be completed orally in its entirety

- ▶ giving written assessments with simplified language

- ▶ administering assessments in smaller portions

- ▶ allowing students to use a dictionary or translating device on tests and/or allowing for extra time or unlimited time

- ▶ not penalizing for spelling or grammar errors (as appropriate)

- ▶ using informal assessment measures such as observational records or oral assessments whenever possible

Reading and English/language arts teachers are in a slightly different position from content area teachers. They must teach basic literacy skills along with the foundations of English as a language students might not be familiar with. Their focus will be on best practices in reading instruction with an emphasis on the needs of English language learners.

Phonemic Awareness: English phonemes are distinct and should be taught explicitly, particularly for sounds that do not exist in the student's native language. However, sounds that are present in the native language and are already known can be transferred rapidly. In this case, instruction in phonemes should focus on those that differ from the student's first language.

Systematic Phonics Instruction: As with all learners, systematic phonics instruction is effective with students whose first language is not English. Decoding through phonics is a two-step process: Teachers must give ELLs the tools to sound out words. But these students must also be able to make meaning of the words based on their oral language vocabulary, which should be developed in tandem.

In addition, automatic word recognition (sight reading) can be very helpful for ELLs. It can speed up reading rate and sometimes prevent difficulties encountered when words deviate from standard phonetic structures.

Fluency: Reading fluency follows oral language fluency. However, ELLs may have trouble with strategies like reading aloud in front of others. They may lack confidence and focus on mistakes instead of growth over time. Oral reading practice with English language learners should be carefully orchestrated, making use of a trusted peer whenever possible.

Vocabulary: Vocabulary instruction for ELLs will vary considerably from their native-speaking classmates. ELLs will need instruction in idioms and basic "connector words" like "because," "and," and so on. They will also need explicit and direct instruction in the vocabulary of the classroom. This includes words frequently used in giving instructions, words associated with subject area, high-frequency words used in speech and texts, and all vocabulary necessary to understand a text. Whenever possible, vocabulary should be taught explicitly and backed up with images or objects.

Comprehension: Comprehension must be carefully scaffolded in a variety of ways. Teachers should provide as much background knowledge as possible to students unfamiliar with aspects of American culture. ELLs, like developing readers, are better able to comprehend text with low complexity. Such texts should be used to build comprehension skills. Graphic organizers, visual aids, and films or multimedia elements to promote comprehension may also be helpful.

Cultural Sensitivity: Awareness of cultural differences is important for all students. It is especially relevant for English language learners, who may be unfamiliar with elements of American culture that many people take for granted. Assumptions about religious beliefs, dietary preferences, clothing choices, family structures, and so on should be avoided. Teachers should select a variety of texts and curricular resources to promote an understanding of diverse cultural perspectives. While many publishers now promote multicultural awareness, teachers should consider curricular resources that include diverse authorial voices.

Sample Question

4) An upper elementary reading teacher is planning a unit on drama that includes a play with advanced vocabulary. How can the teacher best help ELL students achieve success with the play ?
   A.   provide an alternate dramatic text on a different topic for ELL students to read
   B.   encourage ELL students to use context clues as they read the play to identify new vocabulary
   C.   pre-teach important roots and affixes to ELL students to aid in their decoding of new words in the play
   D.   give ELL students a list of words used frequently in the play with their definitions

Students with Reading Difficulties and Disabilities

Legal Issues Related to Reading Disabilities

Today's special education landscape has been shaped by federal legislation over the last fifty years. Before federal legislation mandating school access, many individuals with disabilities were institutionalized rather than given opportunities for education. In institutions, systemic neglect and abuse was common. In the 1960s, alongside other civil rights movements, the disability rights movement raised public awareness of the treatment of individuals with disabilities. The federal government responded with legislation supporting educational opportunities for people with disabilities.

> **Did You Know?**
>
> In 1970, only one in five children with disabilities attended US schools. In fact, many states at that time had laws excluding students with certain disabilities from school.

In 1965, Congress enacted the **Elementary and Secondary Education Act (ESEA)**, which seeks to improve student academic achievement through supplementary educational services as well as increased educational research and training. It also provides financial assistance to schools servicing a high percentage of students from low-income families (Title I funding). ESEA was the first legislation to provide states with direct financial assistance to support the education of students with disabilities.

A major civil rights victory for individuals with disabilities came with the **Rehabilitation Act of 1973**, which ensures all students with disabilities a right to public education. **Section 504** of the Rehabilitation Act prohibits programs that receive federal financial assistance from discriminating on the basis of disability. As federally funded institutions, public schools are required to ensure that students with disabilities receive a comparable education to those without disabilities. If a student with a disability

does not qualify for services under IDEA, they may still receive support through a 504 plan. Under Section 504, students with disabilities may receive related services, accommodations, and modifications to ensure equal access to education.

The most comprehensive civil rights legislation for individuals with disabilities to date is the 1990 **Americans with Disabilities Act (ADA)**. The ADA prohibits discrimination on the basis of disability in the workplace and in all public places (e.g., restaurants, parks, schools, businesses). The passage of the ADA has led to increased community access, accessibility of public transportation, and more equal employment opportunities for individuals with disabilities. As a comprehensive civil rights law, the ADA provides another layer of legal protection for the right of students with disabilities to have equal access to public education.

The first legislation targeting educational rights was the 1975 **Education for All Handicapped Children Act** (EHA, also referred to as **P.L. 94-142**). This act expands educational rights for students with disabilities. The legislation ensures that students with disabilities can access any accommodations, modifications, related services, and specially designed instruction needed to make adequate educational progress in a public school setting.

Congress reauthorized EHA as the **Individuals with Disabilities Education Act (IDEA)** in 1990 and again with amendments in 1997 and 2004. Part B of IDEA provides for services for students between the ages of three and twenty-one, while Part C provides for early intervention services for students from birth to three years old.

Since its original authorization, IDEA has operated under six foundational principles:

▶ **Free Appropriate Public Education (FAPE)**: FAPE maintains that students with disabilities have a right to an education at no additional cost to parents. (Parents of students with disabilities are still responsible for school fees that apply to all students.) The education is required to meet the student's unique educational needs in a public school setting.

▶ **Appropriate and nondiscriminatory evaluation**: Evaluations must be completed by a team of trained professionals (e.g., teachers, school psychologists) and should include information from parents. Evaluations should address all areas of concern, and materials must be sound and nondiscriminatory. Evaluations must be conducted in a timely manner, and reevaluations must occur a minimum of every three years.

▶ **Individualized Education Program (IEP)**: An IEP is a legal document developed by the IEP team (parents, general educators, special educators, administrators, related service providers) that reports present levels of performance, annual goals and objectives, accommodations, modifications, related services, and specially designed instruction to help students make adequate educational progress.

	IEP	Section 504 Plan
Law	Individuals with Disabilities Education Act (IDEA)	Section 504 of the Rehabilitation Act of 1973
Department	Department of Education	Office of Civil Rights
Eligibility	A disability as defined in IDEA that impacts educational performance	A disability that impacts a major life function
Included	Specialized education services, accommodations, modifications, and related services	Accommodations, modifications, and related services
Age	0 to 21 years	No age limits
Location	Schools through grade 12	School through grade 12, college, work

Table 5.1. IEP versus Section 504 Plan

▶ **Least Restrictive Environment (LRE)**: Students with disabilities must be provided supports with nondisabled peers to the maximum extent appropriate for them to make educational progress. This includes access to the general curriculum, which ensures that students with disabilities have access to the same curriculum as their nondisabled peers. LRE emphasizes placement in the general education classroom with supplemental aides and services as much as possible.

▶ **Parent (and student) participation**: Parents must have a shared role in all special education decisions, including IEP reviews, evaluation, and placement decisions.

▶ **Procedural safeguards**: Parents must receive written notice of procedural safeguards, parent and student rights, meetings, and all educational decisions. Parents have access to all student educational records. Parents may take due process measures in the event of a disagreement between the parent and a school district.

The most recent authorization of IDEA is the **2004 Individuals with Disabilities Education Improvement Act**. IDEA 2004 expands procedures for identifying students with learning disabilities to include identification through response to intervention. IDEA 2004 also includes several changes to align with the 2001 **No Child Left Behind (NCLB)** legislation. The main purpose of NCLB is to improve the academic performance of all students through increased accountability for results, emphasizing research-based instruction, and ensuring such instruction is delivered by highly qualified teachers (HQT).

In 2015, Congress passed the **Every Student Succeeds Act (ESSA)** to replace NCLB, effective starting the 2017 – 2018 school year. ESSA rolls back many of the federal education requirements, giving power back to the states. Under ESSA, states are required to create accountability plans, track state-set accountability goals, and incorporate accountability systems (e.g., state assessments, English language proficiency, postsecondary readiness, and school safety). ESSA removes the federal HQT requirement of NCLB. However, each state must set expectations for ensuring HQTs are providing instruction. Moreover, ESSA maintains the state assessment requirements of NCLB and Title I funding for schools.

Sample Question

5) Which of the following would NOT be a service provided to a student under a 504 plan?
   A. occupational therapy
   B. testing accommodations
   C. extra transition time between classes
   D. specially designed instruction

Characteristics of Reading Difficulties and Disabilities

Students progress toward full literacy at different rates. Those who do not meet or are at risk of not meeting grade-level expectations have reading difficulties, which are different from reading disabilities. Students with **reading difficulties** are falling behind grade-level expectations in reading but do not qualify for special education services under the category of specific learning disability (SLD). **Reading disabilities** are formally diagnosed learning disabilities. These students will typically qualify for special education services and are served through an IEP.

Students who qualify for special education services under another category (such as intellectual disability, speech and language impairment or developmental disability) may have other disabilities that cause reading difficulties. Their IEP may list reading-related modifications and accommodations even though they have not been diagnosed with an SLD.

Reading difficulties fall into three categories:

1. **Specific word-reading difficulties (SWD)** describe students who have trouble reading or decoding individual words. They may also have below-average fluency and comprehension levels because they struggle to decode on the word level. When presented with texts they are able to decode, however, these students may have strong reading comprehension skills.

2. **Specific reading comprehension difficulties (SRCD)** are experienced by students who can decode on a basic level but lack the vocabulary knowledge or inferencing skills necessary to comprehend texts fully.

3. **Mixed reading difficulties (MRD)** describe students who have deficits in both decoding and comprehension.

Reading disabilities fall into three categories:

1. **Phonological deficits** occur when students struggle with word recognition due to weak phonological processing. These students face a range of challenges, including trouble with letter-sound correspondence, sounding out words, and spelling. Seventy to 80 percent of students with a reading-related learning disability have phonological deficits. These deficits are usually described by the term **dyslexia**, sometimes called **language-based learning disability (LBLD)**.

2. **Processing speed/orthographic processing deficits** occur when students do not read quickly or accurately. Orthographic coding differs from phonological coding in that it does not rely solely on letter-sound correspondence and knowledge but rather on memory (of letters, groups of letters, or entire words) to decode. This type of deficit is typically milder than a phonological deficit and may be co-occurring or distinct from a phonological deficit. There is some debate as to whether this type of deficit is a subtype of dyslexia or a distinct disability.

> **Did You Know?**
>
> Dyslexia is a very common SLD thought to affect at least 15 percent of the global population.

3. **Specific comprehension deficits** describe issues with vocabulary, language learning, and abstract reasoning. Comprehension deficits might co-occur with phonological or processing deficits as well as with other conditions, particularly Autism Spectrum Disorder (ASD). This type of deficit is also referred to as **hyperlexia** because word recognition skills are average or even advanced.

Sample Question

6) Specific comprehension deficits often co-occur in students diagnosed with
   A. dyspraxia.
   B. dysgraphia.
   C. Autism Spectrum Disorder (ASD).
   D. Emotional Disturbance (EBD).

Assessing Reading Difficulties and Disabilities

Universal screening is an assessment process for possible reading difficulties. It usually takes place three times per year. Schools use different assessment measures for screening, but the most common are:

▶ **Curriculum-Based Measurement (CBM)** is an informal assessment in which a student reads aloud a passage from the core reading curriculum. The student reads for about one to five minutes, while the teacher records the number of words read correctly. This value of number of words correct is compared to the target for the month and year based on predefined standards related to grade and age.

▶ Published measurements include the **Dynamic Indicators of Basic Early Literacy Skills (DIBELS)**, **Woodcock Reading Mastery Test–Revised (WJ–R)**, and **Texas Primary Reading Inventory (TPRI)**. These are more formal assessments that generate more detailed reports than a simple CBM.

Whatever assessment instruments are used to screen for reading difficulties, they should meet the following criteria:

▶ sensitivity: degree to which an instrument detects at-risk students

▶ specificity: degree to which the instrument avoids false positives

▶ practicality: brevity and simplicity of the assessment

▶ consequential validity: refrains from inequity in identification and is shown to lead to effective intervention

Different states, districts, and schools may establish different criteria for labeling students as at-risk for reading difficulties. Some use a threshold measure, for example: "students who score lower than X or who read fewer than X words correct per minute." Others use norm-references such as national or state averages. Still others develop their own criterion and may label performance as satisfactory/unsatisfactory or high-risk/low-risk.

Students identified as at-risk during universal screening should be provided support using the multi-tiered systems of support (MTSS) framework. The student may be referred for evaluation of eligibility for special education services at any point during this process based on school district policy and the student's situation. These services may enable some students to receive more targeted or appropriate interventions than with existing Tier 2 and Tier 3 intervention frameworks.

> **Did You Know?**
>
> Because of the desire to identify all students who might benefit from interventions for reading difficulties or disabilities, some educational researchers believe the rate of "false positive" identification to be as high as 50 percent.

If students are referred for evaluation for special education services, various instruments can be used to determine the presence of reading-related disabilities (including but not limited to dyslexia). These test for skills in phonological awareness; decoding; fluency and comprehension; and rapid naming, a skill linked to reading fluency. Some of these assessment measurements are:

▶ Comprehensive Test of Phonological Processing (CTOPP-2)

▶ Phonological Awareness Test (PAT-2: NU)

▶ Test of Word Reading Efficiency (TOWRE-2)

▶ Gray Oral Reading Test (GORT-5)

▶ Rapid Automatized Naming Test (RAN/RAS)

▶ relevant subtests of the Woodcock–Johnson III (WJIII) or the Wechsler Individual Achievement Test (WIAT-III)

MTSS and referral for special education services are not mutually exclusive. Tier 2 and 3 reading interventions are used for students with reading difficulties whether or not they qualify for special education services. Targeted reading interventions are not meant as a replacement for special education services.

The model for MTSS and/or special education interventions differs among schools. Some schools use a sheltered reading intervention class period for all identified students. The class is made up of students with specific learning disabilities, students with other disabilities that impact reading performance, and students who have reading difficulties but do not qualify for special education.

In another school model, students who qualify for special education services might receive services from special education teachers, while students with reading difficulties receive services from reading interventionists.

Not all schools and districts use an MTSS framework. In some settings, students may participate in less formal types of interventions such as voluntary before- or after-school tutoring, summer school, or summer reading programs.

In any model, teachers and interventionists should use **progress monitoring** to determine the efficacy of interventions. Curriculum-based measurements are the most popular method of progress monitoring. There are many print and digital tools to organize and analyze this information. Additionally, several publishers and education technology companies provide digital platforms for ongoing progress monitoring, usually with a per-student, subscription-based fee.

Analyzing data collected through progress monitoring is a core part of reading instruction,, Based on this data, the educator must determine the best plan of action for each student. This might include collaboration with other professionals such as special educators, ESOL teachers, school psychologists, educational diagnosticians, and so on.

Sample Question

7) Asking first-grade students to write the letters of the alphabet as a screening measure for reading difficulties is ineffective because it
   A. lacks practicality.
   B. relies too heavily on background knowledge.
   C. lacks sensitivity.
   D. relies too heavily on quantitative data.

Instructing Students with Reading Difficulties and Disabilities

Students with reading difficulties and disabilities that impact reading performance need explicit, systematic, direct instruction. This model of instruction and practice should be reinforced across settings. For example, students still mastering letter-sound correspondence can practice with charts or flashcards at home.

Additionally, instruction must be based on each student's needs as revealed through assessment and data collection. Instruction not targeted in this way may be ineffective and/or may only increase student frustration.

Instructional strategies and intervention techniques for students with reading difficulties and disabilities are generally provided either to increase word identification or decoding on the word level or to increase overall comprehension. Specific strategies and interventions are discussed below.

Scaffolding refers to the supports used by teachers or sometimes peers during classroom activities. Scaffolds should be built into all lessons per the Universal Design for Learning (UDL), which states that all students should be able to learn from the same curriculum.

Shaping refers to providing incremental reinforcers and is also helpful in instructing students with reading difficulties and disabilities. As students progress, for example, by memorizing more grade-level high-frequency words, they should receive frequent, positive feedback from educators. This feedback is important for students who struggle with reading, as they may not receive consistent positive reinforcers (e.g., high grades, praise from peers) that other students who excel academically typically receive.

Students with reading difficulties on the word level benefit most from phonics instruction, particularly phoneme blending, phoneme segmentation, and phoneme deletion or substitution practice activities. Synthetic (e.g., Elkonin boxes) or analogy-based phonics approaches (e.g., sorting words into categories based on similarities in structures) are popular instructional methodologies for these students.

Intensive, scripted synthetic phonics programs such as Direct Instruction programs (published under names like *Reading Mastery, Corrective Reading, Horizons,* and *Funnix*) are also empirically based and generally effective. However, there is some controversy surrounding them, as they use principles of behavioral analysis such as stimulus-response-feedback as the primary means of instruction.

Students with reading difficulties on the comprehension level benefit most from instruction and interventions that help them develop metacognition to self-assess understanding and apply strategies to

integrate information and synthesize it with existing knowledge. Such strategies include semantic mapping or other visual organizers; reciprocal teaching); and the **PQ4R method**, an extension of the SQ3R method In the PQ4R method, students preview the reading material, generate questions, and read to answer the questions. After that, they reflect on what they have read, recite or retell from memory what they have read, and then review the material for any missed information.

In addition to the instructional strategies above, students with disabilities that impact reading, like dyslexia, can benefit from certain accommodations. **Accommodations** are changes to materials or instructional methodologies that allow all students to learn the same material as their peers.

► Materials Accommodations

- underlining or highlighting the key words in directions

- chunking assignments or presenting them in smaller increments

- using a glossary or list of key vocabulary terms

- using chapter-by-chapter, page-by-page, or even paragraph-by-paragraph reading guides

- using assistive technology

    o audio recordings or books on tape

    o e-readers or tablets

    o text-to-speech software

► Instructional Accommodations

- clarifying directions through oral repetition and providing a written version

- implementing daily routines to clarify expectations

- providing visual aids whenever possible

- encouraging the use of mnemonic devices

- providing students a hard copy of notes

- implementing frequent review and reinforcement activities at the end of each lesson

- reviewing previously learned concepts at the beginning of a new lesson

- creating opportunities for additional or extended practice

- using peer learning strategies

At times, students with reading disabilities will also need modifications to what they are expected to learn. **Modifications** will usually be listed on the student's IEP and may include a reduced number of questions or items on assessments, different grading criteria, and so on. Reading teachers may collaborate with special education teachers to develop and monitor accommodations and modifications for students with learning disabilities that impact reading performance.

8) A fourth-grade student with dyslexia is very frustrated and feeling overwhelmed by the length of the assigned text the class is reading. What should the teacher do?
   A. have the student read a shortened version of the text
   B. encourage the student to set and stick to a schedule of reading a certain number of pages per day
   C. give the student an audio recording of the text to aid in comprehension
   D. read the entire text aloud in class, asking a different student to read orally each day

High-Achieving Students

Reading teachers frequently offer strategies for students with reading difficulties, but there are also students who need greater challenges. As part of the **Universal Design for Learning (UDL)**, all classrooms should use an approach that meets the needs of all learners and allows all students to access the same curriculum. Teachers can meet the needs of high-achieving students with a pyramid approach to plan lessons.

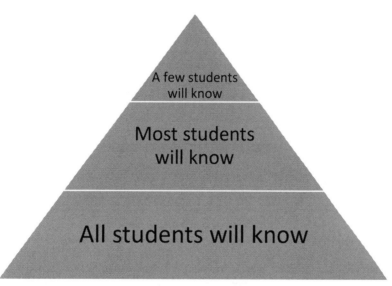

Another widely used model for advanced learners is **Renzulli's Triad Enrichment Model**. This model encourages three types of learning experiences:

1. exploratory opportunities

2. learning experiences in which thinking processes are developed

3. investigative activities

In this model, students typically have some sort of authentic experience with a topic. For example, they might take a field trip to visit a working farm. Then they are instructed on how to research and prepare a multimedia presentation on agriculture in the local community. This empowers them to investigate agriculture in the community and prepare a multimedia presentation.

The following are ways to encourage a love of reading and a deeper exploration of texts by advanced readers in the classroom:

> **Did You Know?**
>
> Not all states mandate specific services for gifted and talented education. What are your state's requirements for gifted education?

▶ Encourage choice of texts. Some students may be ready for more complex texts that are above the Lexile measure for their grade level. These students may find books or passages at grade level boring or redundant. Allowing advanced readers to choose their own materials can encourage them to explore topics of interest and increase engagement. Of course, educators should consider students' reading capabilities and socio-emotional development. Some more complex texts contain mature themes or subject matter that might not be appropriate for younger readers.

▶ Allow for appropriate pacing. Some students may benefit from **acceleration**, or moving through the curriculum at a faster rate than peers. **Curriculum compacting** allows students who have already mastered parts of the curriculum to skip those areas and move on to new material.

▶ Extend learning through independent projects, project-based learning, or other methods that encourage critical thinking and deeper comprehension of texts.

Independent learning is an appropriate enrichment activity for advanced readers, but it does not replace explicit instruction, which high-achieving students also benefit from. Advanced learners should not be given "busy work" or simply be given the entire class period for independent reading.

Reading teachers should work with other teachers as needed to devise enrichment activities that extend *purposeful* learning to enhance and extend the core curriculum. Such activities allow for student choice and exploration of individual interests. For example, in a class reading the novel *Across Five Aprils*, an advanced learner might extend purposeful learning by preparing a presentation on the Civil War and presenting it to the class as part of the introduction of the novel. This keeps the student engaged in class-wide activities and benefits all learners in the classroom.

Sample Question

9) An assignment in which students select a novel and then create a PowerPoint presentation summarizing its plot is appropriate for an advanced reader because it
    A. allows for student choice.
    B. includes elements of technology.
    C. makes use of curriculum compacting.
    D. promotes homogenous grouping.

ANSWER KEY

1) **B.** Lucia is using language chunking and song lyrics to build vocabulary. These are features of early production.

2) **A.** In code-switching, students mix words from their first language in when they speak their second language.

3) **B.** This is a crucial piece of information since ELLs may have experienced disruptions or delays in schooling due to their journey to the United States.

4) **D.** Common Shakespearean words like "thine," "thou," and so on may be new to ELLs. They should be concretely defined before the students read the play.

5) **D.** Specially designed instruction is provided as part of an IEP but not under a 504 plan.

6) **C.** Specific comprehension deficits commonly co-occur in students with ASD.

7) **C.** This assessment measure would not identify students at risk for reading difficulties; it is not sensitive enough. Many students can write the letters but might not, for example, know the sound each letter corresponds with.

8) **C.** Access to an audio recording of the book will help the student feel less overwhelmed and also scaffold comprehension, as the focus is on listening skills versus reading skills.

9) **A.** Research indicates that student choice of reading material is a particularly effective strategy for advanced readers.

6. Assessment and Instructional Decision-Making

Measurement Concepts

Assessment is the process of gathering information from multiple sources to understand what students know. It also measures how they are progressing and if any problems have arisen in their development. Assessment of student learning and progress in reading is ongoing and should occur every school day.

Assessments are conducted in many areas of development, including cognitive, socio-emotional, and physical. Assessments can be used for a variety of purposes:

▶ identifying developmental delays

▶ evaluating student mastery of learning objectives

▶ designing appropriate interventions

▶ gauging efficacy of program delivery

▶ determining placement of students within programs

Data from assessments can then be used to make decisions. These decisions might be related to an individual student, a classroom, or even an entire school or district. Much educational research relies on assessment to yield data that can be applied broadly in other educational situations.

Assessments are ranked based on two factors: reliability and validity. **Reliability** is the rate at which the assessment produces the same outcome every time. One way to think about reliability is in terms of consistency across many different test takers and testing scenarios. A test has low reliability if it does not produce accurate results each time it is given.

Ideally, each assessment would give the same results even when administered multiple times to the same student under the same conditions. Unfortunately, this is not the case. Even assessments that are thought to be reliable have measurement error. **Measurement error** refers to all the variations that impact an examinee's performance. Some variations are testing conditions (e.g., quietness of the room, behavior of the test administrator) or the emotional state of the test taker. Assessments of very young children often have significant measurement error compared to those of older children.

> **Study Tip**
>
> Think of the concept of test reliability as you would a person who is reliable. A *reliable* person behaves as expected every time. A *reliable* assessment instrument does too.

Additionally, many reading assessments conducted in English may contain errors or be ineffective when used with students with limited English proficiency. Particular attention should be paid to matching the assessment to the student needs and intended purpose.

Validity is quite different from reliability. It refers to whether the findings the assessment instrument seeks to measure are accurate and backed by research and evidence. If the assessment does not

measure what it is supposed to measure (achievement, personality, intelligence, or something else), then it lacks validity even if it is reliable and produces consistent results each time.

Assessment data is generally quantitative, or numerical, and qualitative, or nonnumerical. **Quantitative** data is gleaned from standardized assessments such as a numerical IQ or performance in the fifteenth percentile. **Qualitative** data is usually obtained through interviews with parents and teachers and observational records. Both types of data should be considered in initial evaluation for reading interventions or special education services and in ongoing assessment of student learning.

> ### Study Tip
>
> Use the roots of the words to remember quantitative and qualitative data. Quantitative data is a quantity. Qualitative data is the quality of something.

Sample Question

1) A teacher gives a published, criterion-referenced reading assessment instrument to a third-grade student on two different occasions within a week. The student scores much higher on the first assessment. This assessment has measurement error as well as
   A. reliability issues.
   B. validity issues.
   C. a biased norming group.
   D. a small norming group.

Standardized Assessments

There are numerous **standardized** published assessment instruments. These instruments have standardized questions or criteria and are administered in a consistent manner. Most professionals agree that standardized assessments reveal only one part of any student's learning situation and level of mastery of individual objectives. Standardized assessments provide one way to gather data to help with individualized planning and instruction.

Norm-Referenced Assessments

Standardized assessments fall into two categories: norm-referenced and criterion-referenced. Norm-referenced assessments measure an individual student against a group of other test takers, typically those of the same age or grade level. Results are reported in a percentile ranking.

Norm-referenced tests are most often used to measure achievement, intelligence, aptitude, and personality. Achievement tests measure what skills a student has mastered. These often fall under categories like reading and mathematics.

Achievement tests are generally multiple choice and require test takers to answer a standardized set of questions. Popular achievement tests include:

▶ Iowa Test of Basic Skills (ITBS)

▶ Peabody Individual Achievement Test

▶ Wechsler Individual Achievement Test (WIAT-III)

▶ Stanford Achievement Test

Intelligence tests are another norm-referenced assessment. They are used to measure overall intellectual functioning, problem-solving skills, and aptitude for learning. The most commonly used intelligence tests are:

▶ Stanford-Binet Intelligence Scales (SB5)

▶ Wechsler Intelligence Scale for Children (WISC-V)

▶ Woodcock-Johnson III Tests of Cognitive Abilities

▶ Differential Ability Scales (DAS-II)

▶ Universal Nonverbal Intelligence Test (for students with certain communication disorders)

Intelligence tests can help determine giftedness in children and the presence of an intellectual disability. Intelligence tests are also used in tandem with achievement tests to note patterns or discrepancies in IQ and academic achievement. These discrepancies may be the result of a specific learning disability or another condition that might require special services.

> **Did You Know?**
>
> The first exams offered by the College Board (which now produces the SAT) were administered in 1901. The sections were English, French, German, Latin, Greek, history, mathematics, chemistry, and physics. Instead of the multiple-choice format of most of today's standardized tests, questions were in essay format. Student responses were graded as very poor, poor, doubtful, good, and excellent.

Because norm-referenced tests compare students to one another, the results must be given in a format that makes possible such a comparison. The most common way to do this is the **percentile**. A percentile is a score that shows where a student ranks in comparison to ninety-nine other students. For example, a percentile of 81 would mean that the student in question has performed equal to or outperformed eighty-one out of the other ninety-nine students who took the same test. A percentile of 14 means that the student only performed equal to or outperformed fourteen of the other ninety-nine test takers.

These percentiles are usually determined early in the development of a standardized norm-referenced assessment using an early group of test takers known as a **norming group**. Depending on the assessment instrument, these norming groups may be students in a particular school (school average norms) or district (a local norm group). They may also be students with a particular diagnosed exceptionality or special learning situation (special norm group). More often, they are national norm groups. These groups are carefully selected to be representative of the nation as a whole. One criticism of norm-referenced tests is that national norm groups are not always current and truly representative. Students might be taking a test that has not been recalibrated with a new norming group in some time.

Norm-referenced tests base their percentiles on the bell-shaped curve, also called the normal curve or the normal distribution. Often tests are modified so the results will generate a bell-shaped curve. This distribution of scores has three primary characteristics:

▶ It is symmetrical from left to right.

▶ The mean, median, and mode are the same score and are at the center of the symmetrical distribution.

▶ The percentage within each standard deviation is known.

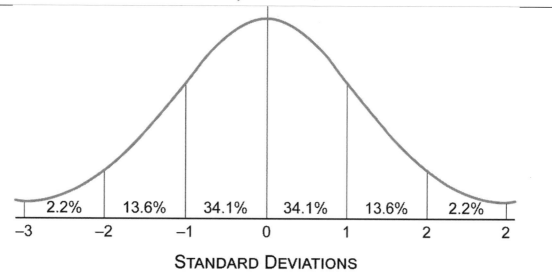

2.2%	13.6%	34.1%	34.1%	13.6%	2.2%

-3   -2   -1   0   1   2   2

STANDARD DEVIATIONS

Figure 6.1. Bell-Shaped Curve (normal distribution)

Not all standardized assessment instruments use percentile. There are also **grade-equivalent scores**, which provide a result in a grade level. This means that the student's performance is equal to the median performance corresponding to other students of a certain grade level. For example, if a student scores at a tenth-grade reading level, that would mean their score was the same as the median for all tenth graders who took the test. Some assessment instruments also use an age-equivalent score, which simply compares a student's results to the median score of other students of a certain age.

Sample Questions

2) Harvey scores in the 89th percentile on the Stanford Achievement Test, an annual norm-referenced test. What do these results mean?
  A. He got 89 percent of the questions correct.
  B. Eighty-nine percent of students did the same as or better than Harvey did.
  C. Harvey did the same as or better than 89 percent of students.
  D. Harvey did well enough to be part of the norming group.

Criterion-Referenced Tests

Criterion-referenced tests measure an individual's performance as it relates to a predetermined benchmark or criteria. These tests are generally used to measure a student's progress toward meeting certain objectives. They do not compare test takers to one another but rather compare student knowledge against the set criteria. Criterion-referenced tests include everything from annual state tests to those created by teachers or educational publishers to assess mastery of learning objectives.

One new incarnation of the criterion-referenced test used by many states is **standards-referenced testing** or **standards-based assessment**. These tests measure a student's performance against certain content standards as defined by each grade level and subject. They are typically scored in categories such as basic, proficient, and advanced; or unsatisfactory, satisfactory, and advanced. Most annual state accountability tests such as STAAR, PARCC, and many others are standards-based, criterion-referenced tests.

Sample Question

3) A reading teacher wants to use the class-wide results of a criterion-referenced test as a starting point to identify levels of vocabulary knowledge among students. Which assessment results should she reference?

A. Iowa Test of Basic Skills
B. annual state accountability test
C. results from a phonics screener
D. results from running records

Types of Assessments

Formal and Informal Assessments

Most programs try to maintain a balance between formal and informal assessment measures. **Formal assessments** refer to test results that are reported in either a percentile or percentage format. Standardized tests, chapter or unit tests, and end-of-course exams are all examples of formal assessments.

Informal assessments evaluate students outside the traditional written test format. These assessments help give a more complete picture of ongoing progress. At times, particularly when students experience stress in high-stakes testing scenarios, informal assessments might provide more accurate results.

Informal assessments include observation, portfolios, projects, presentations, and oral checks, among others. Informal assessment should be ongoing and should guide instruction alongside formal assessment. Informal assessments popular in terms of student literacy development include:

▶ oral reading checks

▶ oral comprehension checks

▶ running records

▶ phonics screeners

▶ exit tickets

▶ informal writing assignments/journaling

Another popular informal reading assessment is the **Informal Reading Inventory (IRI)**. This assessment includes a word list to determine which level of the assessment should be given. It also features an oral reading and silent reading portion. The assessment pinpoints the independent, instructional, and frustrational reading level for each student. The results can then be used to differentiate instruction and choose appropriate reading material for the reading level of each student.

Both formal and informal assessments can be used to gather information and guide instruction. Some students, however, simply do not perform well on formal assessments or may have test anxiety. In these instances, informal assessments are often a better measure of student knowledge.

Sample Question

4) A reading teacher wants to assess student retainment of skills at the end of a small-group intervention aimed at vocabulary acquisition. Which method of assessment should the teacher use?
   A. administer a norm-referenced assessment
   B. ask students to write down three new words they learned
   C. ask students to write three words with long vowel sounds
   D. administer a standardized achievement test

Formative and Summative Assessments

Assessments—whether formal, informal, authentic, or more traditional—can also be either formative or summative. **Formative assessment** refers to the ongoing monitoring of student progress toward learning objectives. Formative assessments are often informal assessments whereby teachers seek more information to streamline instruction. For example, a kindergarten teacher may give frequent formative assessments by asking each student to read words from a sight word list or consonant blend chart. This will help the teacher determine each student's progress in learning to read. It will also provide appropriate and targeted instruction in areas where there is most need.

Study Tip

Formative assessments are used while students are *forming* their knowledge. Summative assessments are used to add up all of student learning into one lump *sum*.

Formative assessments can also be more formal. Examples include a short quiz over the day's material or a concept map or outline that students submit for grading. However, formative assessment tends to be low-stakes assessment: assessment that does not carry a high point value. Formative assessment does not significantly impact a student's course grade or chances of promotion to the next grade.

Summative assessment is designed to evaluate student learning after the end of a defined unit of study. It compares student knowledge to the initial learning objectives that were addressed throughout the unit of study. It, too, may be formal or informal but may often take the form of a unit test, midterm or final exam, or a final paper or project. Summative assessments are generally high-stakes assessments because they carry high point values. They are often critical to a student's overall grade, their ability to pass a course, or promotion to the next grade.

A middle ground between a formative assessment and a summative assessment is the **benchmark assessment**. This type of assessment is more formal than a formative assessment but is not a high-stakes standardized summative assessment. Benchmark assessments are sometimes called interim assessments or predictive assessments. They track student progress and determine the degree to which students are on track to perform well on future summative assessments.

Many states use benchmark assessments before the annual standards-based assessment to determine which students need interventions to help prepare for the high-stakes test. They can also be used to evaluate overall school or district goals and whether the school or district is on track to achieve those goals.

Check Your Understanding

Some districts give benchmark tests up to ten times a year. This has led to some state lawmakers limiting the number of benchmark assessments that can be given each year in hopes of decreasing testing time and increasing instructional time. Does such a law exist in your state?

In some cases, benchmark assessments are less formal. For example, a first-grade teacher using a leveled-reader program may employ a benchmark assessment to determine when her students are ready to move to the program's next level. Similarly, a kindergarten teacher whose goal is to have his students know all the Dolch Sight Words might give them benchmark assessments over smaller sections of the list.

Sample Question

5) A reading teacher gives a daily warm-up quiz with a low point value that covers some of the material discussed the day before. What type of assessment is he giving?

   A. a benchmark assessment

   B. a low-stakes formative assessment

   C. a norm-referenced assessment

   D. a high-stakes summative assessment

Authentic Assessments

One important trend in student assessment is authentic assessment. **Authentic assessment** measures the student's ability to use knowledge in a direct, relevant, often real-world way.

In an authentic literacy assessment, students apply reading and writing skills in a pragmatic or practical way. For example, high school students might work on writing a resume or a profile on a professional networking platform. These are both examples of an authentic assessment of skills in writing for a formal audience. Or, a fifth-grade teacher might give students brochures for places to explore on a field trip and ask them to read and summarize the high points of each brochure. These are authentic literacy assessments since they measure literacy skills in a pragmatic context.

Authentic assessments offer opportunities to go much deeper than a traditional written test. There are numerous examples, many of them cross-curricular, that can be used to assess reading and writing skills in an authentic context. Teachers across multiple disciplines can collaborate to design projects that assess multiple skills. For example, a science teacher and an English teacher might work together to have students research and summarize a scientific article to earn a grade for English and then design an experiment based on the article for a grade in science.

Sample Question

6) A fifth-grade teacher wants to create an authentic assessment to evaluate students' skills with writing in coherent paragraphs. Which assignment would be best?

   A. directing students to give a presentation to the class on something they know how to do well

   B. asking students to analyze the way paragraphs are used in a newspaper article on a topic of their choice

   C. assigning students to write the draft of an email they will eventually send to someone

   D. having students use a graphic organizer to organize their thoughts into paragraphs before writing an essay about an assigned topic

Diagnostic Assessments

Diagnostic assessments are used to determine what students already know. Many teachers give diagnostic assessments at the beginning of the school year or before each unit of study. This helps

calibrate the level of instruction and can help track progress over time when diagnostic assessments are compared with summative assessments.

Diagnostic assessments are particularly important when teachers are implementing pyramid planning as part of the Universal Design for Learning. For example, a teacher discovers through a diagnostic assessment that most of her first-grade students do not know all the letter sounds. It would be unreasonable to expect all her students to be reading sentences by the end of the first unit of study.

Diagnostic assessments can uncover learning gaps that teachers will need to address. For example, a second-grade teacher discovers that many of his students lack knowledge of long vowel sounds. This teacher will need to give explicit instruction in that topic before presenting a unit on spelling that requires students to drop the *e* and add a suffix.

Diagnostic assessments can also be used at the beginning of the year to identify students at risk of not meeting reading learning objectives and to differentiate instruction and plan interventions for these students. Meeting each student at their current learning situation is important in setting goals and targeting instruction.

Sample Question

7) Mrs. El-Badawi is a kindergarten teacher who wants to find out her students' level of phonemic awareness at the beginning of the school year so she can target her instruction. Which is the BEST type of assessment?
A. formative assessment
B. diagnostic assessment
C. summative assessment
D. play-based assessment

Peer, Self-, and Multi-Perspective Assessments

Teachers and parents are not the only ones who can participate in student assessment. Peers can also be very helpful in providing feedback on student learning. **Peer assessment** is the assessment of student work by peers.

Peer assessment is widely used in higher education, particularly in large online classes in which instructors are unable to give feedback on each student's work. If students receive appropriate guidance and practice, peer assessment can be used effectively in many secondary and even some elementary classrooms. While most peer assessment will not result in a formal grade, it can be invaluable to help students revise their work before submitting it for grading.

In a peer assessment, students are given a rubric or list of criteria and asked to assess another student's work based on this rubric or set of criteria. They are also asked to offer specific feedback for improvement. This process can help students who are unsure of how to revise or edit their work, as they are given clear and actionable suggestions.

Peer assessment can also be used during collaborative learning. In this model, the teacher asks for feedback from the group about the level of each member's participation. This can be particularly helpful if much of a group project happened outside of school. This way, the teacher can get some idea of each group member's contributions. This type of assessment is usually more effective when clear criteria for evaluation are set. The teacher might, for example, ask group members to fill out a chart showing which parts of the project each member completed individually and which parts were completed together.

Multi-perspective assessments are also used during cooperative learning activities. In this type of assessment, peers, the individual student, and teachers all collaborate to assess learning outcomes. This can be helpful when parts of a group project occur both in and out of the classroom. In this type of assessment, the teacher may weigh input from different assessors differently when computing the total overall grade. For example, the teacher evaluation of the finished project may count for 75 percent of the grade, the peer assessment of group members for another 10 percent, and the student's self-assessment for the remaining 15 percent.

> ### Did You Know?
>
> Any comprehensive evaluation for special education services will be multi-perspective since a multidisciplinary team, alongside a child's parents, will be participating in the process.

Peer assessment and multi-perspective assessment can be used in conjunction with **self-assessment**. This is a student's evaluation of their individual progress toward learning goals. Self-assessment is a critical part of any child's overall education. It helps students become self-directed learners who devise and meet learning goals with little help from others. Self-assessment should be a large part of formative assessment. Students who are self-assessing can actively seek out the resources they need to meet learning objectives without waiting for teachers to realize they need them.

Usually, self-assessment must be explicitly taught. There are many strategies for this. Often, students are given an example of work that meets certain criteria and then asked to compare their work to this example. In other cases, students are asked to simply assess their degree of understanding of a concept. This could be anything from having students respond in journals or interactive notebooks to prompts such as "Today I learned..." or "I am still unsure about..." Students might use simple symbols like a checkmark or a happy/sad face to indicate their degree of mastery of a given concept.

Sample Question

8) After a group project–based learning assignment, a reading teacher asks each group member to fill out an evaluation of their team members. What method of assessment is this?
   A. peer assessment
   B. multi-perspective assessment
   C. self-assessment
   D. formative assessment

Assessing Emerging Readers

Students who are not yet fluent readers will need specific assessment techniques to ensure they are mastering foundational skills that form the building blocks of later reading instruction. Since concepts of print are the first stage of reading development, these skills must be mastered thoroughly. Most of the time, these assessments are informal and might include any of the following:

▶ asking students to point to the parts of a book (e.g., title, front cover, back)

▶ presenting students with a book and observing as they interact with it

▶ asking students to point to a word, sentence, or picture

As students progress to developing phonetic awareness or overall phonemic awareness, assessment is also conducted in a highly interactive manner. Students might be asked to clap out sounds or words, think of rhyming words, repeat words or sounds, and so on.

Once students begin to work on letter recognition and sound-symbol knowledge, a letter chart or letter-sound chart can be used as assessment tools. Students can cross off each letter or letter sound once it is mastered. The same assessment method with a chart or list can be used for sight words (often with a Dolch Word List), consonant blends, digraphs, diphthongs, and other challenging sounds.

There is an important distinction between children's ability to sing the alphabet song or point to and say letters or sounds in order (which many master quite early) and the different (though related) skill of letter and letter-sound recognition in isolation. For this reason, it is a good idea to always assess phonics skills in different contexts. For example, students can be asked to point to certain letters or sounds (/b/, /ch/, /i/) in a book or story. This type of **embedded phonics** assessment ensures that students can transfer knowledge and apply it in connected texts.

In addition to more structured assessment methods like charts and lists, phonics skills can be assessed through any number of hands-on activities. Students can play with letter/sound cards or magnets and form or dissect words. Students can match up cards with different rimes and onsets or different target consonant or vowel sounds.

In assessing decoding, or the ability to sound out a word and glean meaning, an oral assessment approach continues to be the gold standard. There are many assessment tools designed specifically to aid in assessing such skills, including the popular **Quick Phonics Screener**, which assesses a student's ability to read a variety of sounds and words.

When assessing decoding skills, it is important to note student strengths and weaknesses. But teachers must also develop a general idea of the student's overall approach and "word-attack skills," or methods of decoding unfamiliar words. Attention to how students approach any oral reading task can provide significant information on strategies they are already using, as well as those they do not use but might find beneficial. Though the age of the student certainly comes into play, sometimes older students still mastering decoding might be able to verbalize the way they approach such challenging words. Questions posed to the student about strategy or method can also yield valuable information.

In addition to these methods, there are also several published assessment instruments for pre-readers and emerging readers.

▶ Letter knowledge and phonemic awareness can be assessed using the **Dynamic Indicators of Basic Early Literacy Skills (DIBELS)** and the **Early Reading Diagnostic Assessment (ERDA)**.

▶ The **Comprehensive Test of Phonological Processing (CTOPP)** and **Phonological Awareness Test (PAT)** can also be used as instruments to assess phonemic awareness.

▶ Other instruments that assess early reading skills include the **Texas Primary Reading Inventory (TPRI)**, **Test of Word Reading Efficiency (TOWRE)**, and even the kindergarten version of the **Iowa Test of Basic Skills (ITSB)**.

Regardless of the assessment instruments used, assessing emerging readers can be challenging since young children often find assessment scenarios intimidating. Any single assessment is only as useful as it provides part of the full picture. The fullest picture of a student's pre-reading development can best be gleaned through observation and input from both parents and teachers. Portfolios, observational

records, checklists, and other informal assessment methods can provide much insight into the development of emergent readers.

Sample Question

9) A kindergarten teacher who wants to assess student mastery of phoneme blending would MOST likely
   A. ask students to add affixes to various root words.
   B. have students match up cards with onsets and rimes and say each word.
   C. ask students to remove a letter from a word, add a new one, and read the new word.
   D. have students point to items in the classroom that begin with a certain letter sound.

Assessing Reading Skills and Strategies

Assessing each student in an individual oral context is not always possible. This can make assessing reading skills and metacognitive reading strategies a challenge. Further, it is often hard to fully assess any one student's individual thought process. With these caveats, assessing reading skills and strategies with an eye for gaps that might be addressed through intervention is an important task of the reading teacher.

Word-attack skills can be assessed through observation and oral reading. Teachers should take note of what happens when students encounter words they do not know. Do they immediately ask for help? Skip over the word? Reread the word? Slow down? Speed up? Assessing word-attack skills relies on observation of students as they read aloud but also on the assessment of underlying skills that lead to a strong word-attack tool kit. Do students make use of all text features and graphic elements? Do they sound out the word or make inferences based on roots and affixes? Do they use context clues?

> **Helpful Hint**
>
> Asking comprehension questions after listening to students read is a simple, effective way to monitor oral comprehension.

Assessment of vocabulary typically happens in the context of breadth (the number of words one knows) or depth (the ability to use the vocabulary in varied and nuanced ways). It also happens in the context of an isolated assessment (a vocabulary test) or as an embedded assessment as an adjunct to another assessment, such as one of reading comprehension or oral fluency.

Such assessments can also be context-independent: "What does *contortion* mean?" or context-dependent: "What does the word *contort* mean in the following sentence?" Educators should consider what "bank" they will draw vocabulary from in order to assess students. Typically, teachers assess vocabulary students will need to comprehend the language of classroom instruction, the textbook, and any literature the class will read. Reference materials such as the *EDL Core Vocabularies* define "target" words per grade level. Published standardized vocabulary instruments such as the classic **Peabody Picture Vocabulary Test (PPT)**, which requires no reading or writing, can also be used to assess individual students.

Assessing oral fluency is generally done by assessing reading accuracy, prosody, and automaticity. This can be tracked in numerous ways. Teachers may keep **running records** that track accuracy, self-correction, and use of fix-up strategies and word attack skills. Running records use forms so teachers can mark errors, self-corrections, and how students use cues to make meaning of texts. These forms are filled out as the student reads the same text the teacher has.

Oral fluency can also be tracked using digital tools such as collecting and analyzing recordings of students reading aloud.

Figure 6.2. Running Record

Students can also be measured for oral reading skills using various fluency norms charts that indicate average words read correctly per minute per grade. While several standard measures exist, one of the most researched is the **Hasbrouck-Tindal oral reading fluency chart**. This chart measures progress over the course of the school year and from grade to grade. It compares students in percentiles with their peers on a scale of words read correctly per minute.

Table 6.1. Hasbrouck-Tindal Oral Reading Fluency Chart			
Words Correct Per Minute (50th percentile)			
Grade	Fall	Winter	Spring
1	---	29	60
2	50	84	100
3	83	97	112
4	94	120	133
5	121	133	146
6	132	145	146

Comprehension while reading silently can be assessed through cloze exercises. In these exercises, words are removed from the text and students must fill them in. There are other written exercises aimed at determining level of comprehension. Some students might struggle to answer written questions. Therefore, a full assessment of silent reading comprehension should include an oral component as well.

As previously mentioned, one of the most common assessments is the Informal Reading Inventory (IRI). There are multiple versions created by various entities. One of the more popular versions is **Pearson's Qualitative Reading Inventory (QRI)**. These assessments include oral reading of word lists that assess accuracy of word identification. The QRI also contains passages and questions that assess both oral and silent reading comprehension. Standardized norm-referenced test batteries such as the Iowa Test of Basic Skills and Stanford Achievement Test, as well as several criterion-referenced tests such as the Partnership for Assessment of Readiness for College and Careers (PARCC), also test reading comprehension.

Another popular assessment instrument is called Star. Often used for benchmark data (to see how students are progressing toward meeting objectives), this computer-based assessment includes a built-in tracking and analysis system to help teachers and schools identify students in need of additional support.

However, as in all types of reading assessment, comprehension assessment does not require a lengthy formal written test. Simply asking students to recount or retell a story they have read or to recall the most important or interesting parts of a text can provide valuable data. Further, self-assessment should be ongoing and explicitly taught to all readers to monitor comprehension. As students self-assess, they can apply fix-up or fix-it-up strategies as needed when comprehension breaks down.

Sample Question

10) A reading teacher asks students to skim the text and turn the bold paragraph headings into questions. After the students have read the text silently, the teacher asks them to write answers to each of the questions. What skill is the teacher assessing?

- A. identifying tone
- B. recalling main ideas
- C. activating background knowledge
- D. making inferences

Using Assessment Data

Data from reading assessments can be used in many ways. In schools using a **Multi-Tiered Systems of Support** (MTSS) framework, all students should be screened for reading proficiency early and often. Ongoing assessment (progress monitoring) should be implemented as reading interventions occur.

In an MTSS framework, teachers may conduct universal screenings with any number of assessment tools and then determine which students would benefit from interventions. This data can then be used to determine goals for students identified as "at risk" of not meeting reading objectives. These students will receive early intervening services (Tier 2 intervention) through many possible avenues, though small-group reading instruction is the most common.

As these Tier 2 interventions occur, the teacher and/or interventionist will continue to monitor progress and use assessment data to determine if the student is responding or needs more intensive intervention (Tier 3). This type of intervention is usually in a smaller group and of a greater frequency and longer duration.

When reading teachers are working as co-teachers or as direct providers of intervention services, they will also use assessment data to:

▶ differentiate instruction for all students (Tier 1 interventions) including but not limited to:

- assessing the independent, instructional, and frustrational reading levels for each student and selecting appropriate texts

- providing scaffolds and supports for individual students per the principles of the Universal Design for Learning (UDL)

- using data for flexible grouping strategies that group students by skill level for optimal instruction but constantly reassess and adapt based on student progress

▶ plan and conduct small-group interventions (Tier 2 or Tier 3) by:

- assessing skill gaps where students need additional instruction or practice

- grouping students for interventions based on similar instructional goals/learning needs (keeping in mind principles of flexible grouping)

Assessment data can and should also be used on a macro level to make improvements to instruction and support teachers across the content areas. A reading teacher might use reading assessment data in a variety of contexts, such as:

▶ determining individual classrooms/grade levels that might need additional support

- ► determining grade-level or school-wide curricular needs

- ► determining efficacy of classroom/grade-level or school-wide curricular or intervention approaches

- ► designing intervention approaches or teacher support systems on a school-wide level

- ► recognizing trends across grade levels (e.g., students are not adequately prepared for instruction on spelling words with *r*-controlled vowels at the beginning of second grade)

- ► providing planning or instructional recommendations to teachers

- ► identifying teachers or classrooms to serve as mentors

- ► planning topics for professional development events

The way assessment data is used on a school-wide level will vary, but these are some of the most common uses of such information.

Sample Question

11) After reviewing the data from annual standards-based assessments, a reading teacher sees that results show most third- and fourth-grade students are struggling with the meaning of homographs. Which area of instruction would be best to focus on to aid students in determining the meaning of homographs?

    A. roots and affixes

    B. graphophonic cues

    C. context clues

    D. analogy-based phonics

ANSWER KEY

1) **A.** Reliability refers to how often the test gives the same result. This test clearly has some issues with reliability, as the student should score with similar results on multiple assessments in a short time frame.

2) **C.** Harvey's score was equal to or better than 89 percent of students to whom he is being compared.

3) **B.** Most annual state accountability tests are standards-based assessments that are criterion-referenced based on state standards. This would help the reading interventionist phrase the needs in a concrete and standards-aligned way.

4) **B.** This is a short, informal assessment that gives the teacher the needed data about what has been retained from the session.

5) **B.** A daily warm-up quiz is a low-stakes formative assessment. It is designed to be an ongoing monitoring of student learning and has a low point value.

6) **C.** This assignment is authentic assessment because students will actually send the email to someone, so the assessment has a real-world application. It also allows the teacher to assess the students' use of paragraphs.

7) **B.** A diagnostic assessment will help Mrs. El-Badawi determine her students' existing knowledge of phonemic awareness.

8) **A.** Students assessing other students is peer assessment.

9) **B.** When students say the onset and rime together, they are blending both phonemes together.

10) **B.** The paragraph headings and the questions generated from them are clues to the main idea of each paragraph. Asking students to answer the questions requires them to recall main ideas from the text.

11) **C.** The context of the sentence in which the homograph is written will clue its meaning. Instruction in looking for context clues will aid students in determining the meaning of these types of multiple-meaning words.

Practice Test 1

Phonological and Phonemic Awareness/Emergent Literacy

1) A prekindergarten teacher notices one of her students, Rene, is pretend reading a book from the back cover to the front cover. Which of the following does Rene need more practice with?
   A. phonemic awareness
   B. phonological awareness
   C. letter-sound correspondence
   D. concepts of print

2) Which of the following statements is true about phonemic awareness?
   A. It generally has to be explicitly taught.
   B. It is natural and intuitive.
   C. Most students will master it at the same rate.
   D. Students do not need it to begin reading.

3) Anna has just joined a teacher's first-grade class. She and her family recently moved from Taiwan to the United States, and they speak little English, especially Anna. The teacher knows that her home language is Mandarin, and she knows that its sounds are often very different from English sounds. The teacher is spending the bulk of the allotted reading time on phonics decoding and word-attack skills. Most of the class is working on spelling words with challenging consonant digraphs like –ch, –sh, and –th. In what way might the teacher differentiate instruction for Anna, who does not yet speak English fluently?
   A. give her a book to read in Mandarin while the rest of the class is working on spelling
   B. have her copy the spelling words instead of writing them independently
   C. avoid any phonics instruction and focus on developing Anna's English vocabulary
   D. design an activity that will help Anna become familiar with basic English phonemes

4) Which of the following categories describes a common way to classify phonemes?
   A. vowel versus consonant
   B. morphology versus semantics
   C. receptive versus expressive
   D. generative versus procedural

5) How many morphemes does the word "painted" have?
   A. one
   B. two
   C. three
   D. four

6) A kindergarten teacher says to a student, "We study at the li/brar/y. Where do we study?" This activity is designed to promote which of the following?
   A.   phoneme blending
   B.   phoneme segmentation
   C.   awareness of orthographic pattern
   D.   concepts of print

7) Using texts with alliteration can help young children develop which of the following?
   A.   oral automaticity
   B.   phonemic awareness
   C.   pre-phonetic spelling
   D.   digraph recognition

8) Which of the following word pairs shows both a CV and VC pattern?
   A.   *on, go*
   B.   *off, pin*
   C.   *clap, up*
   D.   *big, bad*

9) Mrs. Ramirez has a classroom routine of conducting a read-aloud with her kindergarten class each morning and then asking her students questions to gauge their level of comprehension, engagement, and interest in the story. Which of the following types of questions should Mrs. Ramirez primarily ask her students?
   A.   rhetorical questions
   B.   open-ended questions
   C.   closed-ended questions
   D.   passive-listening questions

10) Which of the following words cannot be spelled through simple phoneme segmentation?
   A.   up
   B.   bigger
   C.   not
   D.   help

11) Which of the following words has the onset italicized?
   A.   pl-*ate*
   B.   *br*-oom
   C.   in-*ter*-est
   D.   fair-

12) A kindergarten teacher notes that a student struggles to remember the sounds letters make. What kind of exercises would best benefit this student?
   A.   those aimed at graphophonemic skills
   B.   those aimed at print awareness
   C.   those aimed at orthographic processing
   D.   those aimed at phonological processing

13) A teacher has her first grade students complete a journal page every day. They draw pictures and write descriptions of their pictures, spelling the words as well as they can.
How does this activity contribute to students' phonics proficiency?

    A.   Students connect letters to sounds.
    B.   Students practice authentic decoding.
    C.   Students build fine motor skills.
    D.   Students identify orthographic patterns.

14) Which of the following words contains a digraph?
    A.   sap
    B.   cat
    C.   hay
    D.   go

Phonics and Decoding

1) A teacher notices that Eva, one of her kindergarten students, is trying to read the following sentence:

The ball sits.

Eva can sound out the words *ball* and *sits* but is struggling with the word *the*. Which of the following targeted practice should be used with Eva?
    A.   give her more practice with challenging digraphs like *th*
    B.   give her more practice with letter-sound correspondence
    C.   have her practice more silent reading and less oral reading
    D.   give her practice with high-frequency sight words

2) Which of the following is true of beginning phonics instruction that might occur in a kindergarten classroom?
    A.   It usually involves lots of oral exercises.
    B.   It relies heavily on sight word knowledge.
    C.   It presumes students have a knowledge of Latin and Greek roots.
    D.   It does not require knowledge of letter-sound correspondence.

3) A second grade teacher wants to improve students' decoding skills. Which of the following would be the most effective instructional strategy?
    A.   introducing character analysis
    B.   teaching word families
    C.   encouraging finger tracking
    D.   demonstrating think-alouds

4) Which of the following letters is most likely to be introduced first in progressive phonics instruction?
    A.   a
    B.   g
    C.   y
    D.   m

5) To determine a student's proficiency with letter-sound correspondence, which assessment instrument would be most appropriate?
   A.   cloze
   B.   Dolch word list
   C.   maze
   D.   nonsense word list

6) A first-grade teacher is introducing open syllables. Which word would she use as examples?
   A.   because
   B.   least
   C.   total
   D.   stir

7) What is the definition of graphophonemic knowledge?
   A.   Students know that phonemes change when word endings change.
   B.   Students know that words are made of letters that represent sounds.
   C.   Students know that syllables are divided at phoneme boundaries.
   D.   Students know that reading and spelling are interconnected.

8) Students should be taught which of the following rules about vowel teams?
   A.   They always make a long vowel sound.
   B.   They make a single vowel sound.
   C.   They always make a schwa sound.
   D.   They always come in words with more than one syllable.

9) A reading teacher directs students with the following: "Say the word *tray* without the /t/." By which age would a typically developing child be able to respond correctly to this direction?
   A.   4
   B.   5
   C.   6
   D.   8

10) A reading teacher is working with a small group of first-grade students who are just entering the full alphabetic phase of word reading. Which types of words is the teacher most likely to use for guided practice?
   A.   CCVCC
   B.   CVC
   C.   VCC
   D.   CCCVC

11) One advantage of using connected texts as part of beginning phonics instruction is
   A.   exposing students to high-frequency sight words
   B.   gleaning accurate student Lexile reader measures
   C.   encouraging students to use evaluative comprehension
   D.   helping students identify worthwhile mentor texts

12) Students who rely solely on graphophonic cuing will most likely
   A.   read with automaticity
   B.   read with greater comprehension
   C.   read more slowly
   D.   read more frequently

13) A third-grade teacher wants to encourage students to be more independent and self-directed readers. A lesson on which topic would best meet this goal?
   A.   fix up strategies
   B.   prosody
   C.   graphic organizers
   D.   orthography

14) One advantage of phonics over whole language instruction is that students
   A.   sound out words versus guessing
   B.   memorize a huge bank of words
   C.   seek out and use environmental print
   D.   work independently instead of as a class

15) A second grade student is able to identify and say the first and final sound in several CVC words, but not the middle sound. During interventions, which concept should the teacher practice with the student?
   A.   long vowels
   B.   consonant blends
   C.   diphthongs
   D.   short vowels

16) Which existing sound would students need familiarity with before they are introduced to the schwa sound?
   A.   long e
   B.   short a
   C.   short u
   D.   long i

Comprehension of Literary and Informational Text

1) Reading texts used for direct instruction or guided instruction should be at
   A.   the student's independent reading level.
   B.   the student's frustrational reading level.
   C.   the student's instructional reading level.
   D.   the target Lexile level for the grade above.

2) A reading teacher is seeking a resource for teaching students metacognition as they read. Which of the following resources would meet this goal?
   A.   a list of self-reflective questions
   B.   an oral fluency assessment rubric
   C.   a bundle of leveled readers
   D.   a chart of digraphs and vowel teams

3) A reading teacher working with a small group of students asks them to use each of the bold headings in their textbook to generate questions they will answer after reading the chapter. This is a strategy to help students do what?
- A. read with purpose
- B. activate background knowledge
- C. apply fix-up strategies
- D. use context clues

4) Which of the following is an evaluative question that a student might ask while reading?
- A. How many pet cats did Celeste have?
- B. What might happen to Celeste's cats?
- C. What do I think about Celeste as a person?
- D. How old is Celeste?

5) One advantage of texts in a digital format is that they
- A. can be read at a faster rate.
- B. may have multimodal elements.
- C. are always up to date.
- D. are written at a lower level of complexity.

6) Which activity would best help second-grade students begin to summarize texts?
- A. written retellings
- B. language experience approach (LEA)
- C. QAR strategy
- D. SQ3R strategy

7) A teacher selects a poem with the following lines to use in guided practice with fifth grade students.
hungrily she gobbled down
the creamy gravy thick and brown
without a thought she munched so loud
her teeth chomping violently drew a crowd

This stanza can be used for instruction in which of the following topics?

- A. figurative language
- B. free verse
- C. sensory imagery
- D. alliteration

8) A reading teacher is working with a small group of third grade students on identifying theme. Which of the following self-guiding questions should the teacher have students ask themselves?
- A. What did I like best about this story?
- B. Why did I read this story?
- C. What is the author trying to teach me in this story?
- D. How is the author different from others I have read?

9) Students who need help confirming inferences they have made from the text should do which of the following?
  A. reread the text
  B. determine the text structure
  C. critique the text
  D. cite evidence from the text

10) Poetry written in free verse would not be amenable to assessment items written to test identification of which of the following?
  A. figurative language
  B. symbolism
  C. tone
  D. meter

11) Which of the following is a qualitative text measure?
  A. mean sentence length
  B. word count
  C. average word length
  D. knowledge demands

12) The main goal of a K-W-L chart is to help students
  A. organize new vocabulary based on similar semantic and syntactic qualities.
  B. use a set framework for activating background knowledge, setting a purpose, and summarizing.
  C. refer to a set list of fix-up strategies and then choose the most appropriate one for the situation.
  D. learn how to make inferences, identify purpose, and distinguish between fact and opinion.

13) Which of the following statements BEST describes an effective reading curriculum?
  A. It is based on incidental phonics instruction.
  B. It is explicit and systematic.
  C. It contains digital texts.
  D. It is continuous from kindergarten through twelfth grade.

14) A third grade teacher encourages her students to check out and read books on any topic of interest and helps students identify books appropriate for their current reading level. The most important benefit of this approach is that students can:
  A. read independently without the need for teacher scaffolding
  B. learn new vocabulary via implicit means
  C. use authentic materials as mentor texts
  D. begin developing the habit of reading for pleasure

15) A third grade teacher wants to help ELLs write a summary of a story. Which strategy is most likely to be effective?
  A. helping students identify text evidence for key conclusions
  B. providing sentence frames like First,_____. Next,_____. Last,_____.
  C. giving students a word list of transitional expressions like *thus, furthermore,* and *also.*
  D. reviewing the difference between simple and complex sentences.

16) A third grade teacher wants to help a reader struggling with comprehension select a book for independent reading time. Which type of book should the teacher direct the student toward?
- A.   a story with flashbacks and foreshadowing to drive interest
- B.   a nonfiction book with a word pronunciation guide
- C.   a book of rhyming poetry
- D.   a fiction book with a simple plot

17) Which of the following is an example of an informational text?
- A.   poetry anthology
- B.   short story
- C.   novel
- D.   brochure

18) Mr. Smith's second-grade class is going to read a story aloud. He wants to emphasize that the narrator has a different point of view from the other characters. Which of the following should he do to emphasize this point?
- A.   read the entire story himself and point out when the narrator is speaking
- B.   have students read in a different voice when reading/speaking as the narrator versus when reading/speaking as the characters
- C.   have students label the text for each line that is spoken by the narrator
- D.   have students read very slowly when reading the narrator's lines so they can really appreciate the narrator's points

19) Mark, a third grader, is having difficulty identifying the main idea of texts he reads. Mrs. Martinez wants to give him extra practice with this skill when he completes his weekly oral reading assessment. Which of the following is the best way for Mrs. Martinez to incorporate the identification of the main idea into Mark's weekly oral fluency assessment?
- A.   stopping him after he reads each paragraph and asking, "What was that paragraph about?"
- B.   assigning him longer passages to read so that he can practice with more advanced texts
- C.   having Mark read only nonfiction texts since the main idea is easier to identify
- D.   giving Mark passages with varying themes so that he has more exposure to different genres

20) Which of the following describes the role exposition plays in a story?
- A.   It sets up the setting and characters.
- B.   It allows the climax to unfold.
- C.   It is the sequence of events leading up to the climax.
- D.   It ends the story.

21) A teacher wants to plan an integrated literacy and science activity to engage his second-grade class in increasing their visual literacy. Which of the following activities would be most appropriate to meet his goal?
- A.   an activity where students find an image or graphic online about recycling and then explain what the image communicated
- B.   an activity where students organize and implement a school-wide recycling effort
- C.   having students read a short story about a boy who is praised for recycling
- D.   having students conduct thorough research both online and at the school library to find out more about types of products that can be recycled

22) A student in a fifth-grade reading class is finding the identification of the story's climax to be a challenge. Which graphic organizer is most likely to help?
- A.   character map
- B.   outline
- C.   word web
- D.   plot diagram

Writing Skills and Processes

1) A teacher working with a small group of students uses a sample from a textbook that illustrates conventions of letter writing. This text is BEST described as which of the following?
- A.   mnemonic device
- B.   literary guide
- C.   mentor text
- D.   phonogram pattern

2) A fourth-grade teacher is reading through student journals. Though the journals are given a grade based on completion, what else should the teacher consider to help guide future instruction?
- A.   gaps in student knowledge of punctuation and mechanics
- B.   possible presence of undiagnosed disabilities
- C.   need for targeted handwriting instruction
- D.   any code-switching or use of a specific dialect or register

3) A teacher observes a prekindergarten student write the following on a piece of paper at the classroom's writing center:

3R TTT AB

This student is MOST LIKELY in which of the following developmental stages of writing?
- A.   scribbling
- B.   transitional writing
- C.   invented spelling
- D.   preconventional

4) A fifth-grade reading teacher researches pre-writing strategies. Which of the following strategies is she MOST LIKELY to use?
- A.   COPS mnemonic
- B.   predict-o-gram
- C.   semantic impression
- D.   RAFT method

5) A fifth-grade teacher gives students words from a story the class will read and then asks them to write their own story using these words. Which of the following strategies is the teacher employing?
- A.   neurological impress
- B.   predict-o-gram
- C.   word experts
- D.   semantic impressions

6) A fourth-grade teacher considers multiple strategies to help ELL students navigate the writing process, particularly the revising and editing phase. Which of the following strategies should the teacher use?
   A.   encourage ELL students to read their work aloud to check for grammatical errors
   B.   pair ELL students with peers whose first language is English during writing conferences
   C.   allow ELL students to type their essays and use the spell-check feature
   D.   provide heavy scaffolding to include the teacher directly identifying errors for the student

7) A pre-kindergarten student cannot write her name independently, but after drawing a self-portrait, she asks her teacher to write her name as a model so she can copy it onto her drawing. This student is demonstrating which of the following?
   A.   phonemic awareness
   B.   procedural knowledge of writing
   C.   conceptual knowledge of writing
   D.   cognate awareness

8) A second-grade teacher wants to build student writing skills as well help them develop basic skills in summarization. Which of the following activities BEST meets her goals?
   A.   written retellings
   B.   neurological impress
   C.   shared writing
   D.   word experts

9) Which of the following would make the greatest impact on students' writing abilities?
   A.   inviting professional writers to share their experiences with the class
   B.   setting aside time each day for sentence diagramming and oral drill
   C.   having students write only about topics they care about deeply
   D.   allowing time for writing each day or during each class

10) A third grade teacher gives each student a checklist to compare their personal narrative against before submitting. Which of the following skills is the teacher helping students to develop?
   A.   self-assessment
   B.   fix-up strategies
   C.   transactional reading
   D.   guided writing

11) The authoring cycle is referred to as a recursive process because
   A.   writers go through the steps in a strict logical sequence.
   B.   writers may have to return to a previously completed part of the process.
   C.   multiple modalities are used to create meaning in writing.
   D.   proficiencies are developed only very gradually with much sustained effort.

12) A third grade teacher asks students to submit possible topics for an informative essay. One student submits the topic of "television." What is the BEST feedback for the teacher to provide?
   A.   think about how to narrow the focus
   B.   develop a pro/con list based on the topic
   C.   focus on gathering primary sources
   D.   begin with an outline to guide drafting

13) Writing instruction in early kindergarten usually focuses on which of the following?
   A.   semantics and morphology
   B.   spelling remediation
   C.   the alphabetic principle
   D.   syntax and mechanics

14) Which of the following describes the BEST way for a kindergarten teacher to integrate technology into the writing process?
   A.   teaching students to use the spell- and grammar-check feature in word-processing software
   B.   structuring research assignments that require students to search online databases
   C.   using software that allows students to drag and drop pictures to create a story
   D.   allowing time each day for students to complete online punctuation drills

15) A fourth grade student has completed a data dump pre-writing exercise with the topic of "benefits of cats." What should she do next?
   A.   use her word list to prepare an outline
   B.   think of synonyms for each of the words
   C.   draft her essay using all the words
   D.   select the best words from the list

16) Which of the following assessment methods would be MOST effective to gauge student writing progress over time?
   A.   norm-referenced assessment
   B.   criterion-referenced assessment
   C.   dynamic assessment
   D.   portfolio assessment

Vocabulary and Fluency

1) After a student completes a reading fluency assessment, the teacher notes that he reads all words correctly but with great effort, sounding out each phoneme. Which part of fluency does he need further practice and instruction with?
   A.   prosody
   B.   automaticity
   C.   decoding
   D.   pragmatics

2) A first-grade teacher wants a technique to help students with automatic word recognition. Which of the following techniques should the teacher employ?
   A.   neurological impress
   B.   sustained silent reading (SSR)
   C.   reader's theater
   D.   curriculum-based assessment (CBA)

3) In working with students to develop overall comprehension and fluency, teachers should encourage them to adjust their reading rate based on which of the following?
   A.   level of interest
   B.   current grade level
   C.   presence of rhyme
   D.   text complexity

4) A reading teacher plans to follow the Universal Design for Learning (UDL) with ELLs. Which of the following scaffolds is the BEST to use?
   A.   pull-out instruction on cognate awareness
   B.   a supplemental curriculum designed for ELLs
   C.   excusing ELL students from collaborative learning activities
   D.   allowing students to use a picture dictionary or electronic translator

5) Which assessment technique would most effectively measure a student's expressive vocabulary?
   A.   having the student point to the picture that matches a spoken word
   B.   asking the student to describe her family or some topic about which she is familiar
   C.   having the student read a paragraph containing many new words aloud
   D.   asking the student to write down as many words as possible in a two minute period

6) A fourth grade teacher uses the Frayer Model in both reading and content-area instruction. How is this tool helpful to students?
   A.   aiding in vocabulary acquisition
   B.   teaching fix-up strategies
   C.   aiding in annotation of key details
   D.   teaching synthesis of information throughout the text

7) A second grade teacher is using running records to track oral reading fluency. In addition to tracking skipped words, repeated words, and other errors, the teacher assigns a holistic score of 1, 2, or 3 as an assessment of student expressiveness while reading. This primarily focuses on which aspect of reading fluency?
   A.   automaticity
   B.   rate
   C.   prosody
   D.   decoding

8) A first grade teacher introduces new vocabulary each week by projecting the word, its definition, and a picture to the class. However, the teacher is concerned that students are not retaining this vocabulary knowledge. Which instructional strategy is most likely to help?
   A.   giving a written assessment immediately after the lesson
   B.   using the vocabulary words as the weekly spelling words
   C.   repeatedly using the words in context in her speech throughout the week
   D.   intentionally teaching students the root and etymology of each new word

9) A second grade teacher is modeling fix up strategies for students. As the teacher gets to a certain part of the text she says "Oh....I don't know much about this....and the words look pretty hard." What should the teacher say next?

A. "I probably need to slow down my reading speed here."
B. "I had better start over from the beginning."
C. "I think I should look for text evidence to make an inference."
D. "I need to find a different text that will be easier."

10) Which strategy should be used to help a third grade class access a content-area text that contains many unfamiliar words?

A. having students annotate unknown words as they read
B. providing explicit instruction in new words beforehand
C. teaching students to preview the text for new words
D. helping students divide the words into syllables

11) A reading specialist is collecting data on foundational literacy skills in a kindergarten classroom. She observes an English language learner complete the following exercise:

Directions: Read the word aloud. Then circle the picture that matches the word.

BALL

The student sounds out the word correctly as /b/ /a/ /l/ but then circles the picture of the bug. Which of the following conclusions might the reading specialist draw?

A. The kindergarten teacher is not providing systematic phonics instruction.
B. The student has recognized a false cognate.
C. The student may need further vocabulary instruction.
D. The kindergarten teacher is not providing sufficient instruction in phonemic awareness.

12) A fifth-grade teacher plans a lesson on digital dictionary skills. What type of vocabulary instruction is being provided?

A. incidental vocabulary learning
B. word-learning strategies
C. semantic impressions
D. semantic features analysis

13) A second-grade reading teacher is concerned that some students sound out every word they encounter even if they know the word. This slows down reading rate and impacts overall fluency. Which of the following strategies is MOST appropriate for the teacher to employ?

A. switch to a phonics through spelling approach
B. encourage students to preview texts and circle known words
C. have students skip over known words as they read orally
D. focus on developing a semantic cuing system

14) A third grade reading teacher wants to give students strategies to better comprehend new words they encounter in their science textbook. Which of the following strategies is the MOST appropriate to use?
- A. providing students with a thesaurus to refer to as they encounter new vocabulary
- B. teaching students some of the most commonly used roots and affixes for content-area words
- C. encouraging students to read fiction texts on similar topics that feature content-area words
- D. giving students a brief refresher on the basics of the graphophonic cuing system.

15) Which of the following words has a prefix?
- A. antihero
- B. goldsmith
- C. graciousness
- D. understandable

16) Which assessment technique would most effectively measure a student's expressive vocabulary?

- A. having the student point to the picture that matches a spoken word
- B. asking the student to describe her family or some topic about which she is familiar
- C. having the student read a paragraph containing many new words aloud
- D. asking the student to write down as many words as possible in a two minute period

17) A third grade teacher wants to focus on explicit vocabulary instruction with Tier 2 words. Which group of words is most appropriate to use for such a lesson?

- A. try/tries/tried
- B. metamorphosis/metacognition/metanarrative
- C. found/help/gone
- D. ability/determine/reasonable

18) A second grade teacher wants to help students develop strategies to understand what new words mean based on syntactic cuing. The teacher has just introduced the words *beauty*, *invent*, and *trace*. Which activity best meets this goal?
- A. Students write sentences using the new words and note their position in the sentences.
- B. Students practice with new forms of the words such as *beautiful, inventive,* and *traced.*
- C. Students identify antonyms of the words such as *ugly, idle,* and *freehand.*
- D. Students work to activate background knowledge by asking questions like "What similar word do I know?"

19) A student who struggles with fluency due to sounding out each individual letter sound is likely in which of Ehri's four phases of word reading?
- A. pre-alphabetic
- B. automatic
- C. full alphabetic
- D. partial alphabetic

20) A sixth-grade teacher plans to give students a text that includes some archaic language such as "thou" and "heretofore." Which vocabulary learning strategy is likely to be MOST effective?
   A. identification of base words and affixes in the words
   B. pre-teaching the words ahead of time
   C. using a thesaurus while reading
   D. allowing use of a picture dictionary

21) In a paired reading exercise aimed at developing fluency, students should be placed in
   A. homogenous groups
   B. student-choice groups
   C. heterogeneous groups
   D. mixed-age groups

Constructed Response

1) A third-grade student is asked to read the sentences that follow as part of a diagnostic assessment.

Sentence	Student's Reading
Children like to bring their dogs to parks on weekends.	Cil-d-ren like to be-ri-n-gu-h their dogs to p-aa-r-k-z on we-ki-n-d-s.
Parents enjoy time with pets, too.	Pa-r-e-n-tz un-joy t-ime with pets, too.

- Describe TWO skills this student has most likely mastered with specific evidence from this assessment to back up assertations.

- Describe ONE skill the student requires more support to develop with specific evidence from this assessment to back up the assertion.

2) A fifth-grade teacher notices that students do well on discreet vocabulary assessments that involve matching words to definitions, but students struggle with Tier 3 vocabulary in content-area texts that they read.

- List TWO recommendations for vocabulary identification strategies the teacher could teach students and why these would help students with these texts.

- Suggest ONE concrete instructional activity the teacher could employ to help students master EACH vocabulary identification strategy.

3) A fourth-grade teacher has three ELL students enrolled in the class. The school uses a structured literacy approach with frequent formative and summative assessments. The teacher wants recommendations for accommodations she can make to these assessments aligned with the Universal Design for Learning (UDL).

- Describe ONE accommodation the teacher can make to a writing assessment along with a detailed rationale.

- Describe ONE accommodation the teacher can make to a reading assessment along with a detailed rationale.

Answer Key 1

Phonological and Phonemic Awareness/Emergent Literacy

1) **D.** Rene understands that books are to be read, but she may not yet understand they have a clear order of beginning, middle, and end. The other choices relate to the use of sounds and the sounds letters make.

2) **A.** Phonemic awareness does not come naturally. This is why people who cannot read can.

3) **D.** Anna is likely unfamiliar with many of the forty-four English phonemes, and she will need practice with these before tackling more advanced activities such as the consonant digraphs the rest of the class is working on.

4) **A.** Phonemes can be categorized by vowel versus consonant.

5) **B.** Paint + ed is two morphemes. Morphemes are the smallest units of meaning in words. Endings that indicate tense or singularity or plurality are considered morphemes.

6) **A.** Phoneme blending exercises ask students to make words out of sounds.

7) **B.** Recognition of repeated sounds is part of overall phonemic awareness.

8) **A.** *On* is a VC and *go* is a CV pattern.

9) **B.** Open-ended questions yield a response beyond a yes or no; these will encourage her students to think more deeply about the story.

10) **B.** Students would have to know to double the consonant *g*, and simply sounding out the word *bigger* would not generate the correct spelling.

11) **B.** The onset is the initial consonant sound, in this case the blend *br*.

12) **D.** Phonological process includes phonological awareness, phonological memory and phonological retrieval, so these exercises would be most relevant.

13) **A.** Emergent writing activities such as journaling provide students with opportunities to connect the sounds they hear in words to the letters representing those sounds.

14) **C.** In the word *hay*, –*ay* is the digraph. A digraph is two letters making a single sound.

Phonics and Decoding

1) **D.** *The* is a high-frequency sight word and must be memorized versus sounded out.

2) **A.** Phonics involves connecting written language to spoken sounds.

3) **B.** Word family instruction is a decoding strategy that reinforces student understanding of word patterns.

4) **D.** The letter *m* is most likely to be introduced first because it contains its sound in its name and only forms one sound in words.

5) **D.** Having students read nonsense words ensures that they can sound out all letter sounds and are not reading by sight memorization.

6) **A.** Be-cause has an open first syllable. It ends in a vowel and make a long vowel sound.

7) **B.** Graphophonemic knowledge is also sometimes referred to as the alphabetic principle.

8) **B.** Vowel teams are two vowels that make a single sound like "treat."

9) **D.** Phoneme deletion from a blend like /tr/ is a challenging skill that is typically not mastered until age 8 or 9.

10) **B.** Consonant-vowel-consonant words are the least difficult words to read and require only knowledge of each isolated letter sound. Thus, these words would be appropriate for students who just learned all the letter sounds.

11) **A.** Connected texts such as short stories or passages will also contain high-frequency sight words, which students will not be exposed to when completing exercises with target "phonics words" presented in isolation.

12) **C.** Graphophonic cuing is the least efficient manner of decoding because it relies on matching letters and sounds. Thus, students who are solely using this system will read more slowly and likely more laboriously.

13) **A.** These are strategies students can use to decode unknown words and when their understanding of words or connected texts breaks down. Having a "toolbox" of such strategies can help students become more independent and self-directed as they read.

14) **A.** Phonics instruction emphasizes sounding out words, while whole language instruction emphasizes memorization of words and may lead to guessing about unknown words.

15) **D.** CVC words have a short vowel sound in the middle, so this would be the best focus for this student who seems to know consonant letter sounds but not vowel sounds.

16) **C.** Schwa sounds are sounds that make a short /i/ or short /u/ sound.

Comprehension of Literary and Informational Text

1) **C.** Texts at the instructional reading level should be used for most direct instruction and guided instruction. These texts are challenging but still manageable.

2) **A.** A list of self-reflective questions like "Do I understand?" or "How much do I understand?" could help students with metacognition as they read.

3) **A.** Having set questions will help students to read with the purpose of answering these questions.

4) **C.** Asking this question allows readers to form an opinion about Celeste, which makes it an evaluative question.

5) **B.** One advantage of digital texts is that they might contain audio and video that help communicate across different modes.

6) **A.** Written retellings have young students write a few sentences about what they have read.

7) **C.** This stanza appeals to the senses of sight, taste, and sound.

8) **C.** The theme is the message or lesson that the author is trying to teach.

9) **D.** Students should be able to identify the part of the text that led them to an inference or conclusion.

10) **D.** Free-verse poetry is "free" of structural elements of poetry like rhyme and meter.

11) **D.** This is the only measure that is qualitative, or based on qualities of the text, versus quantitative. Knowledge demands refers to background information students will need to comprehend a text successfully.

12) **B.** Students use a framework to activate background knowledge ("what I already know"), set a purpose for reading ("what I want to know"), and summarize what they have learned ("what I learned").

13) **B.** Any effective reading curriculum is explicit and systematic, meaning it is direct, unambiguous, and follows a clear and logical order.

14) **D.** These students are likely to become lifelong readers. The more a student reads, the more proficiently the student will read.

15) **B.** This will help students by providing a framework so they are not simply writing ex nihilo.

16) **D.** Genre is one factor that influences comprehension. A story with a simple and predictable plot will likely be most accessible to a student still developing comprehension.

17) **D.** A brochure is a nonfiction text without characters that gives the reader information. The other options are fictional, not informational, texts.

18) **B.** This will help students understand that the narrator is telling the story from a different point of view.

19) **A.** This will give Mark extra practice identifying the main idea during oral reading assessments.

20) **A.** The exposition, or the beginning of the story, sets up the reader for what is to come by describing the setting and main characters.

21) **A.** Visual literacy is the ability to comprehend visual texts, so this activity would give students

22) **D.** The plot diagram shows the climax as the "high point" of the story, which may help this student visualize.

Writing Skills and Processes

1) **C.** A text that students use as a sample to aid in writing in a certain format, style, organization, or particular feature is a mentor text.

2) **A.** Knowing student skill gaps will help the teacher target instruction.

3) **B.** Transitional writing is characterized by spaces between groups of letters that are the first attempt at writing words.

4) **D.** The RAFT method has students ask what the role of the writer will be, who the audience will be, what format will be used, and what topic will be presented.

5) **D.** Students using semantic impressions compare the story they have written with the story they have read.

6) **B.** Having ELLs review their work with a peer whose first language is English is an effective way to use homogenous grouping and actively involve ELLs in the revision process.

7) **C.** The student is demonstrating an understanding that the letters of her name will label the picture. This is an understanding of the concept of writing in that it is used to communicate meaning.

8) **A.** With written retellings, students retell a story they have read in a shorter form in their own words.

9) **D.** Writing as much as possible is one of the best ways to improve writing ability.

10) **A.** Students are being encouraged to reflect on their writing and self-assess it based on established criteria.

11) **B.** In the revision process, for example, writers might have to return to the pre-writing or drafting stages.

12) **A.** "Television" is too broad a topic for a paper, so the best feedback is to think about how to narrow the focus.

13) **C.** By using the alphabetic principle, students begin to understand that written language is part of a "code" in which letters stand for certain sounds that create meaning.

14) **C.** This is a developmentally appropriate way to integrate technology into the writing process. Even before students are able to write in the most traditional sense, they can experience the writing process by selecting images to insert into the story.

15) **D.** After a data dump, students can refine their list by circling the most closely associated words or crossing out unrelated words.

16) **D.** A portfolio shows student progress over a span of time. Writing samples will hopefully show growth and increased proficiency and complexity.

Vocabulary and Fluency

1) **B.** The student needs to practice recognizing and reading words effortlessly and automatically.

2) **A.** In neurological impress, an adult and child read the text together, while both point to the words. This is thought to "etch" the words into the mind of the learner and help improve automatic word recognition.

3) **D.** When students read a challenging text or a challenging part of a text, they should slow down their reading rate to maintain comprehension.

4) **D.** A picture dictionary or electronic translator would allow ELLs to participate fully in activities by helping them with vocabulary.

5) **B.** Expressive vocabulary refers to the words that students are able to use in speech or writing, so this assessment technique would be most appropriate.

6) **A.** The Frayer Model is a four-part diagram that helps students break down a vocabulary words in terms of its definition, characteristics, and examples and non-examples.

7) **C.** Prosody refers to the expressiveness of oral reading.

8) **C.** This helps students generalize this knowledge and hear the words being used in context. It balances explicit vocabulary learning with implicit vocabulary learning as they hear the words being used in an authentic context.

9) **A.** This is a common and useful fix up strategy. When texts are complicated or contain lots of new information, slowing down the reading speed can be highly effective.

10) **B.** Pre-teaching new vocabulary, particularly in a content-area text, is likely to drive student comprehension.

11) **C.** The student was able to sound out the word, but not fully decode it for meaning since the student did not correlate the sounds with the meaning of "ball."

12) **B.** Being skilled at using a dictionary helps students to learn new words as they encounter them.

13) **B.** By having students preview text and circle words, they can just say the sight words when they come to them instead of sounding them out.

14) **B.** Morphemes like "bio" and "evo" and many others can help students as they encounter content-area words.

15) **A.** *Anti–* is a common prefix that means *opposite of* or *against*.

16) **B.** Expressive vocabulary refers to the words that students are able to use in speech or writing, so this assessment technique would be most appropriate.

17) **D.** Tier 2 words are frequently used words that are essential for students' progress in school. These words are such words that are also appropriate for grade three students to learn.

18) **B.** Syntactic cuing is structural cuing, so students would work on the structure of the words. These new endings make words that are different parts of speech but have similar meanings to the known words.

19) **C.** In this phase, students know all the letter sounds but are not yet recognizing phonics patterns. Thus, they still sound out each letter sound individually, which can be laborious.

20) **B.** Pre-teaching these words before students are exposed to the text is the best course of action because these words will not at all be familiar to students, making the other options unlikely to help students actually understand the meaning of the words in context.

21) **C.** Such an exercise is typically most effective when more fluent readers can serve as models for less-fluent readers.

Constructed Response

1) SAMPLE ANSWER

This student has mastered letter-sound correspondence because he or she is able to correctly sound out (though laboriously) most words with very basic phonics patterns like "parks" and "parents." He is even able to read very basic CVC words like "dogs" and "pets." The student has also developed fluency with many high-frequency sight words like "to," "their," "on," and "with."

However, in words with more advanced phonetic structures, the student struggles. Consonant blends are a particular problem as the student is sounding out each sound in the blend instead of the entire blend together. For example, the student does not say /br/ but instead says /be-ri/ in "bring". Additionally, the student says /n-guh/ instead of and /ng/ in the word "bring" and /n-t/ instead of /nt/ in "parents." To help the student advance in fluency, instruction in common consonant blends is recommended.

2) SAMPLE ANSWER

The teacher could help students employ morphological analysis. This would help students with content-area words because such words often have common roots such as geo-, mono-, tri-, etc. Another strategy that could help these students is previewing text features because such vocabulary words are likely to be bolded in the textbooks and likely even contain pronunciation guides and perhaps links to a glossary.

To practice morphological analysis, students could be trained on a "known-word" strategy. This would involve identifying a word part that is known and then making an inference about the new word. For example, students likely know that "tri" means "three" from the word "triangle." When faced with the word "tribunal" in a social studies text, they can identify "tri" and infer that "three" people are involved. To practice using text features the teacher could model a previewing "think-aloud" of a content-area text chapter. The teacher would speak aloud his or her internal monologue such as: "I see bold words, so these words must be new....Do I know this word? No...I better look it up in the glossary first then..."

3) SAMPLE ANSWER

One accommodation to a writing assessment would be to allow the students to submit written essays in smaller chunks, such as individual paragraphs, for feedback instead of submitting the entire essay at once. ELL students may have limited expressive vocabulary, so writing pieces of great length may be more time-consuming than for students who speak English as a native language. Additionally, submitting essays in chunks would allow for the teacher to give specific, targeted, actionable feedback for students to apply before submitting the next segment. Such an accommodation allows all students to write the same essay aligned with the principles of UDL.

For reading assessments, one accommodation would be to allow ELL students to use a dictionary. This would ensure that the assessment is really gauging comprehension. Often ELL students struggle with English vocabulary as the first barrier to comprehension. Scaffolding these students by allowing them to look up unknown words on reading assessments would ensure that limited vocabulary knowledge is not the reason for a low score or for missing certain questions. This also aligns with the principles of UDL because all students can still take the same assessment.

Practice Test 2

Phonological and Phonemic Awareness/Emergent Literacy

1) Mark, a first-grade student, is sounding out the word *flat*. He sounds out the word *f-l-a-t*. Which of the following is true about Mark?
- A. He is lacking basic knowledge of the alphabetic principle.
- B. He needs more practice with affixes.
- C. He sounded out each letter individually versus the onset and rime.
- D. He has a strong knowledge of consonant blends.

2) Mr. Scott writes the following words on the board:

blimp

roar

grin

He asks his class to make a new word out of each word by removing a part of the existing word. Which of the following concepts is the teacher trying to develop in his students?
- A. the alphabetic principle
- B. phoneme deletion
- C. phoneme substitution
- D. phoneme segmentation

3) Storybook reading with pre-readers helps to develop oral language skills in which of the following ways?
- A. It increases knowledge of vocabulary and syntax.
- B. It helps students practice expressive communication.
- C. It exposes students to diverse orthographic patterns.
- D. It promotes phonemic awareness and letter-sound correspondence.

4) A first-grade teacher gives her students the following cards:

Br	im
Sw	ead

She then asks them to connect the cards to make words. Which of the following concepts does this activity reinforce?
- A. phoneme deletion
- B. onset and rime
- C. receptive vocabulary
- D. long vowel sounds

5) Which of the following activities BEST assesses knowledge of letter-sound correspondence for kindergarten students?
- A. timing students as they recite the alphabet
- B. timing students as they read from a sight word list
- C. checking off known phonemes from a chart
- D. checking off known letter names from a chart

6) A prekindergarten teacher wants to expose students to a variety of sources of environmental print. Which of the following materials would be MOST effective?
- A. leveled readers
- B. signs and labels
- C. Elkonin boxes
- D. letter-sound charts

7) Which of the following questions would be most appropriate to help prereaders identify the conflict in a story?
- A. Who are the characters on this page?
- B. How was the problem resolved?
- C. Why was (character name) so mad?
- D. Where did this story happen?

8) Mrs. Ray has just read *The Three Little Pigs* to her class. She then divides her kindergarten class into three groups. She tells the first group to draw a picture showing the houses of the pigs. She tells the second group to draw a picture of the wolf trying to blow the houses down. She tells the third group to draw a picture of the wolf falling into the pot of boiling water. She then asks the class which group's pictures come first, second, and last. What is Mrs. Ray's overall goal for her students with this activity?
- A. Mrs. Ray wants to check that her students understand the descriptions of the pigs and wolf.
- B. Mrs. Ray is having her students practice describing the setting of a story.
- C. Mrs. Ray is helping her students understand the organization of the story.
- D. Mrs. Ray wants to reinforce key vocabulary from the story.

9) A kindergarten class has a spelling center where students use letter magnets to spell out the names of different objects based on a picture card. Johnny has just spelled *dog* with the magnets correctly placed under the picture of the dog. The teacher comes by and says to Johnny, "Let's read this word together, /d/ /o/ /g/. What word did I sound out?" Which of the following concepts is the teacher trying to help Johnny develop?
- A. onset and rime
- B. phoneme segmentation
- C. phoneme blending
- D. phoneme deletion

10) Mr. Hawks wants to give his kindergarten students a sight word assessment. Which of the following is the best way to conduct this assessment?
    A.   direct the students to write the sight words from memory
    B.   ask students to read from a sight word list while he circles the words they know
    C.   have students sound out each sight word as he presents it to them
    D.   encourage students to clap out the beat as they repeat each word after him

11) How many phonemes are there in English?
    A.   26
    B.   44
    C.   18
    D.   15

12) A student in a first grade class is struggling to sound out basic CVC words because of phonological deficits. What will this student most likely also find difficult?
    A.   print awareness
    B.   encoding
    C.   previewing
    D.   listening skills

13) During the first week of first grade, a teacher gives a diagnostic assessment asking students to read a list of five simple CVC words. One student is unable to sound out any of the words. What action should the student's teacher take?
    A.   determine if he knows the name of each letter
    B.   assess his knowledge of individual letter sounds
    C.   give the assessment again with picture cues
    D.   ask him to write any words he can read

14) A kindergarten teacher wants to help students go beyond literal comprehension as she reads a storybook to the class. Which guiding question best meets this goal?
    A.   Who is the main character?
    B.   What is the character's name?
    C.   What happened first in the story?
    D.   What do you think will happen next?

Phonics and Decoding

1) Which type of diagnostic assessment would give a first-grade reading teacher the most information on students' knowledge of consonant blends?
    A.   a group activity in which students take turns placing letter tiles in boxes for each phoneme
    B.   a whole-class choral reading activity in which students read a paragraph with multiple consonant blends
    C.   an individual assessment with a phonics screener or similar targeted list of words and sounds
    D.   an activity in which students write down the sounds they hear while words are read aloud

2) A second grade student asks a teacher: "Why do the words *say* and *weigh* have the same sound but a different spelling?" The teacher could use this question as a starting point for a mini-lesson on:
   A.   letter-sound-correspondence
   B.   morphophonology
   C.   graphemes
   D.   homographs

3) A student is able to orally substitute the initial consonant /g/ for /b/ in the word *boat* to make the word *goat*. What concept is the student demonstrating?
   A.   phonemic awareness
   B.   letter-sound correspondence
   C.   phonological awareness
   D.   manipulation of onsets and rimes

4) Which group of words contains words with r-controlled vowels?

   A.   bread/bring/craft
   B.   robin/race/rub
   C.   torn/curb/bird
   D.   try/dry/fry

5) A third-grade teacher wants to model the process of metacognition during reading as a precursor to fix-up strategies. Which question would she most likely use?
   A.   What genre is this?
   B.   How are the characters developed?
   C.   Do I understand this paragraph?
   D.   Where can I learn more about this topic?

6) A first-grade teacher gives a list of words with CCVC patterns for an integrated decoding and encoding lesson. Which word would appear on the list?
   A.   what
   B.   stink
   C.   awful
   D.   shy

7) Which of the following best describes the research on systematic phonics instruction with English language learners?
   A.   less effective than a whole-language approach
   B.   effective when combined with vocabulary instruction and automatic word recognition
   C.   effective when combined with an emergent phonics curriculum that evolves with student interest
   D.   less effective than an embedded phonics approach

8) A second-grade teacher is introducing a unit on diphthongs for an integrated reading and spelling unit. Which word would appear on the list?
   A.   tree
   B.   cluster
   C.   drive
   D.   through

9) Which activity is most aligned with an explicit, systematic phonics approach?
  A. Students learn phonics rules by encountering them in authentic texts.
  B. Students work in cooperative teams to investigate phonics rules.
  C. Students are taught to use picture cues as the first method of decoding.
  D. Students are given teacher-directed instruction in decoding strategies.

10) Which word-solving strategy would be most appropriate for students still developing automaticity?
  A. identifying roots and prefixes
  B. looking for vowel-consonant-e patterns
  C. using context clues to confirm word meaning
  D. focusing on words with irregular spellings

11) Which of the following activities is a multisensory approach to phonics instruction?
  A. Students use the same list of words for reading and spelling.
  B. Students form and say words with consonant blends in the sand.
  C. Students participate in both guided and independent practice.
  D. Students progress to more advanced sound patterns in a defined scope.

12) An upper elementary student who struggles to decode basic CVC words may have which type of reading challenge?
  A. Specific comprehension difficulty
  B. Processing speed deficit
  C. Specific word- reading difficulty
  D. Hyperlexia

13) Which shows a logical progression of the least to most difficult introduction of phonics patterns?
  A. r-controlled vowels, short vowels, long vowels
  B. letter sounds, consonant blends, vowel teams
  C. digraphs, diphthongs, letter sounds
  D. closed syllables, onset-rime, long vowels

14) A kindergarten student is struggling to segment words into syllables. Which instructional resource would best aid this student?
  A. word family cards
  B. picture sorts
  C. letter puzzles
  D. Elkonin boxes

15) A student who is proficient in most phonics patterns will need instruction or introduction to which concept before he or she will be able to read with prosody?
  A. context clues
  B. syllable types
  C. punctuation
  D. orthography

16) Recursive phonics instruction should include
- A. repetition
- B. spelling
- C. active learning
- D. ability grouping

Comprehension of Literary and Informational Text

1) A fourth-grade teacher wants to activate students' background knowledge before reading a nonfiction passage on space exploration. Which of the following activities BEST meets this goal?
- A. asking students to freewrite a story set in outer space with extraterrestrial characters
- B. having students construct a Milky Way galaxy out of construction paper and glitter
- C. having students think about careers of the future that may be possible because of space exploration
- D. asking students to write down three things they know about space exploration

2) A teacher brings in a nature magazine, a thesaurus, a novel, and a history textbook. As he holds up each text, he asks students why they might read each. This is MOST LIKELY an anticipatory set for a lesson on which concept?
- A. making inferences
- B. choral reading
- C. setting a purpose
- D. identifying text structure

3) A third-grade student is always first to finish his independent reading work, but he consistently misses many comprehension questions that require inferencing. Which of the following strategies should his teacher recommend?
- A. making better use of graphophonic cues
- B. using a dictionary when needed
- C. reading texts at the instructional level
- D. slowing down the reading rate

4) Which of the following is the MOST appropriate text for independent reading for most fourth-grade students?
- A. a poem at a Lexile level of 1200
- B. a nonfiction text at a Lexile level of 770
- C. a drama at a Lexile level of 1100
- D. a fiction text at a Lexile level of 200

5) A character map would be an appropriate semantic organizer for which of the following types of texts?
- A. a nonfiction passage about snails
- B. a poem about the beauty of nature
- C. a short story about a young girl
- D. an argumentative essay about school uniforms

6) Before assigning a historical fiction novel, what should the reading teacher do to give students the necessary background knowledge?
- A. reveal the climax and resolution
- B. provide students with a character trait chart
- C. encourage students to determine the theme
- D. give insights into the setting

7) How are the central idea and topic of a nonfiction text related?
- A. The topic is what the author is saying about the central idea.
- B. The topic and the central idea are identical.
- C. The central idea is much broader than the topic.
- D. The central idea is what the author is saying about the topic.

8) To introduce the idea of general story structure or plot diagram, which type of text would be most effective?
- A. a fairy tale
- B. a biography
- C. literary nonfiction
- D. a novel told in flashback

9) Comparing a fiction and nonfiction text on the same topic can help students to do which of the following?
- A. increase overall knowledge of morphology
- B. develop skills in identifying logical fallacies
- C. recognize differences among genres
- D. modify prosody based on audience

10) A student reading a text at around 85 percent accuracy with at least 75 percent comprehension is reading at the
- A. independent reading level.
- B. instructional reading level.
- C. frustrational reading level.
- D. career readiness reading level.

11) Students in a fifth grade social studies class read a primary and secondary source on the same topic and then compare the two texts. Which foundational reading skill is the teacher helping students to develop?
- A. activating background knowledge
- B. drawing reasonable conclusions
- C. making connections
- D. annotating the text

12) In which situation would a reading teacher use an Informal Reading Inventory (IRI)?
- A. to assign students to a particular small reading group
- B. to determine students' progress toward end-of-year objectives
- C. to assess whether students have a specific learning disability related to reading
- D. to screen for developmental delays in speech and language

13) Why has universal screening for reading difficulties become standard practice for most elementary schools?
   A. It allows for a more systematic process of selection of a reading curriculum.
   B. It provides further data to support the efficacy of phonics instruction.
   C. It can identify at-risk students for prompt early intervention.
   D. It allows paraprofessionals to take a more active role in reading assessment.

14) A lesson in a second grade classroom on prereading strategies is most likely to involve which topic?
   A. morphology
   B. predicting
   C. evaluative comprehension
   D. phonological processing

15) A third grade teacher gives students a reading journal where students set goals, track the books they've read over the course of the year, and write a few sentences about each book after they've finished it. The primary purpose of this strategy is to:
   A. encourage students to read more books than peers
   B. interest students in books on diverse topics
   C. help students become self-directed learners
   D. assess how students are meeting state standards

16) A second-grade teacher in upstate New York is reading a short story designed for children that is set in mid-nineteenth-century Georgia. Which of the following should be discussed with students to help them better understand the story?
   A. the way the short story switches between different registers
   B. the content-specific words students may be unfamiliar with
   C. the dialogue from characters who speak in a different dialect
   D. the reasons people in the nineteenth century did not speak properly

17) Which of the following is a structural element of literature?
   A. point of view
   B. prosody
   C. fiction versus nonfiction
   D. main idea

18) Mrs. Hayball is reading a story to her kindergarten students as part of an integrated unit on community leaders. The book is about a girl whose mother is running for mayor. About halfway through the book, the election happens. At this point, Mrs. Hayball stops and asks the following question: "What do you think is going to happen?" Which of the following skills is Mrs. Hayball helping her students practice?
   A. building anticipation
   B. making predictions
   C. integrating curriculum
   D. understanding character motivation

19) Which of the following activities would be appropriate when introducing the idea of a summary to a first-grade class?
   A. having students write a summary for each paragraph in their social studies textbook
   B. asking the class to brainstorm several phrases and ideas that describe the story overall
   C. identifying the point of view of each story they have read and keeping this information in a journal or notebook
   D. asking the students several questions orally about each character's motivation

20) Which of the following is typical of a narrative written in first-person point of view?
   A. The author is a minor secondary character.
   B. The audience does not know what the protagonist is thinking.
   C. The author is the narrator and protagonist.
   D. The author puts the reader in the role of protagonist.

21) A teacher has a group of gifted and talented first-grade students. He sets up the classroom with several tables full of different types of reading material. He has newspapers, magazines, books, brochures, letters, and more. He tells his students to explore these materials and think about what makes them different from each other. He asks them to think about the presence or absence of pictures, size of the print, organization, and other features. Which of the following skills is the teacher most likely trying to develop in his students?
   A. the ability to read and understand a wide variety of texts on many different reading levels
   B. the ability to select texts that are most appropriate for their own reading level
   C. the ability to compare information presented in different forms
   D. the ability to compare digital and physical print

22) Which of the following questions should a teacher ask to assess literal comprehension?
   A. Where did the story take place?
   B. What can you infer about the main character?
   C. Would you want to be a character in the story? Why or why not?
   D. What new vocabulary words did you find in the story?

Writing Skills and Processes

1) Which of the following words would be appropriate for a preschool child to use as a practice word to begin copying letters from an environmental source?
   A. the word *blimp* as dictated to her
   B. the child's name written on a piece of paper for her to copy underneath
   C. the word *McDonald's*, which she retains the spelling of from memory
   D. the word *elephant*, which she writes after she is shown a picture of an elephant

2) Research has shown that teaching English grammar and mechanics through isolated drill leads to
   A. marked improvement in overall student writing capabilities.
   B. little to no improvement in student writing.
   C. an increase in student revising and editing skills.
   D. a greater student ability to provide constructive feedback during editing.

3) While helping a fourth-grade student revise his essay, a teacher notices that the student has used slang and regional dialect throughout. Which of the following is the BEST course of action for the teacher to take?

    A.   Review the fundamentals of proper English and have him rewrite the essay.

    B.   Encourage him to think about the fundamental differences between speaking and writing.

    C.   Ask him to consider his audience and revise the essay using more formal language.

    D.   Provide time to give him more explicit instruction in grammar and mechanics.

4) A third-grade teacher giving a high-quality lesson on homophones. However, the teacher has planned a traditional fill-in-the blank spelling test as the only assessment of student learning after the lesson. What type of assessment should the teacher give instead to help students generalize knowledge?

    A.   Have students write a paragraph using several homophone pairs correctly.

    B.   Include homophones as part of a class-wide oral spelling bee to encourage students to further study the words.

    C.   Ask students to study a high-frequency homophone list for a few minutes each day at home.

    D.   Extend the lesson by having students examine the morphology of the homophones.

5) Which of the following writing strategies would be MOST beneficial for students with physical disabilities that impact fine motor skills?

    A.   framed paragraphs

    B.   data dump

    C.   shared writing

    D.   interactive writing

6) Words selected for spelling lists should be at the student's

    A.   frustrational reading level.

    B.   instructional spelling level.

    C.   independent spelling level.

    D.   instructional reading level.

7) A fifth grade reading teacher wants to find strategies to integrate reading and grammar instruction. Which of the following strategies should the teacher pursue?

    A.   combining instruction in pronouns with point of view

    B.   combining instruction in diagramming sentences with making inferences

    C.   encouraging students to critique the way authors create a mood through word choice

    D.   encouraging students to fuse together sentences from a short story to make run-ons

8) A teacher hangs a poster in the classroom that says, "*I* before *E* except after *C* or when sounded like *ay* as in *neighbor* and *weigh*." This poster gives an example of

    A.   a continuum of spelling.

    B.   a graphophonic cue.

    C.   a phonogram.

    D.   an orthographic pattern.

9) A fifth-grade teacher suggests that students should read aloud pieces they have written. The teacher is MOST LIKELY suggesting this because

    A.   students of this age are still developing oral language skills.

    B.   the teacher should grade writing only after hearing it read aloud.

    C.   this is a simple way for students to publish their work.

    D.   oral reading is the optimal time for mechanics instruction.

10) While observing writing conferences in an upper elementary classroom, a teacher hears a student suggest to a peer that he delete an irrelevant sentence from his essay. The teacher would MOST LIKELY praise the student for her suggestion to improve the essay's

    A.   tone.

    B.   organization.

    C.   style.

    D.   focus.

11) A teacher writes the following list on an elementary classroom board:

Long A	Short A
paper	apple
danger	catwalk
grape	scan

Which of the following spelling activities is the class MOST LIKELY engaged in?

    A.   cover-copy-compare

    B.   segmentation

    C.   word sorts

    D.   word families

12) Which of the following strategies is most useful for helping students develop coherence and organization in their writing?

    A.   freewriting or journaling

    B.   DR-TA

    C.   RAFT

    D.   framed paragraphs

13) A student receiving literacy interventions writes the following introductory paragraph for his autobiographical essay:

My name is Joel my friends sometimes call me Joe. I have lived in Boston all my life I enjoy baseball fishing and marshal arts. After school. I live in a large house my two brothers live there to.

Which type of targeted mechanics instruction should the teacher providing interventions plan?

    A.   basic orthography

    B.   sentence structure

    C.   basic capitalization

    D.   preposition use

14) Peer review activities can be an effective part of the writing process when they
    A.   occur within a structured framework.
    B.   use homogenous grouping.
    C.   encourage brutal honesty.
    D.   take place without teacher assistance.

15) In which type of writing would students be MOST LIKELY to use a dialect or register and still communicate a message effectively?
    A.   an expository essay
    B.   a free-verse poem
    C.   a research paper
    D.   a biographical essay

16) Purposeful instruction in the mechanics of writing should focus on which of the following relationships?
    A.   mechanics and communication
    B.   semantics and pragmatics
    C.   inductive and deductive reasoning
    D.   mechanics and vocabulary

Vocabulary and Fluency

1) Which strategy would be most helpful for a fourth-grade teacher who wants to help her students develop prosody?
    A.   audio-assisted reading
    B.   analytic phonics
    C.   reader's theater
    D.   reading workshop

2) A fourth-grade teacher uses timed repeated readings to help students build fluency. Which type of texts should she select for such readings?
    A.   unfamiliar texts
    B.   poetry only
    C.   familiar texts
    D.   fiction texts only

3) A fourth-grade teacher wants help students build oral fluency. Which of the following strategies is the MOST LIKELY to meet this goal?
    A.   paired reading in heterogenous groups
    B.   reciprocal teaching in homogenous groups
    C.   think-alouds that promote metacognition
    D.   cloze exercises completed independently

4) Jenine is a second-grade student targeted for extra reading practice. One day, the teacher listens to her read a paragraph out loud and notices that Jenine is reading very slowly. Which of the following parts of fluency does Jenine need help with?

    A.   rate

    B.   prosody

    C.   accuracy

    D.   phonemes

5) What is the purpose of sight word instruction in an elementary classroom?

    A.   to help students learn letter-sound correspondences to improve accuracy

    B.   to help students manipulate sounds in words to improve auditory skills

    C.   to help students recognize words automatically to improve fluency

    D.   to help students use word parts to improve reading comprehension

6) A second grade teacher has a student with dyslexia in the general education classroom. The student often struggles with losing her place while reading a connected text. What strategy is most likely to help this student?

    A.   use of audio texts

    B.   teaching fix up strategies

    C.   text annotation

    D.   finger tracking

7) To help students expand their vocabulary based on root words they already know, they can be instructed in:

    A.   common derivational morphemes

    B.   etymologies

    C.   creating and using word walls

    D.   syllabication

8) A student in a first grade class is struggling with oral fluency. The teacher believes some of the issue may involve the student's lack of confidence. Which strategy should the teacher try?

    A.   modeling appropriate rate and prosody

    B.   having the student participate in reader's theatre

    C.   giving the student a familiar text for oral assessments

    D.   encouraging the student to segment sentences

9) As part of a vocabulary exercise, a fourth grade teacher allows students to draw a picture representing each word, write a sentence demonstrating the meaning of each word, or audio or video record a conversation of them using each word. This activity best shows this teacher's commitment to:

    A.   standards-based assessment

    B.   universal design for learning

    C.   inquiry-based learning

    D.   criterion-referenced assessment

10) A third grade teacher begins a unit on affixes like -ive, -ion, and -ly. What other topic could be easily integrated into this unit?
    A.   academic language
    B.   sentence structure
    C.   parts of speech
    D.   active and passive voice

11) A reading teacher conducting a curriculum-based measurement (CBM) determines that a third-grade student is reading at a rate of 150 words correct per minute. What next step should the teacher take?
    A.   refer the student for evaluation for special education eligibility
    B.   identify possible enrichment opportunities for the student
    C.   place the student in a cohort for Tier 2 interventions aimed at developing fluency
    D.   place the student in a cohort for Tier 3 interventions aimed at developing fluency

12) An upper elementary teacher has several English language learners who need additional vocabulary development practice. Which of the following strategies would be most appropriate?
    A.   teaching fix-up strategies
    B.   using a language experience approach (LEA)
    C.   instruction in common idioms
    D.   incidental vocabulary learning

13) Why do young English language learners need vocabulary development activities alongside synthetic phonics instruction for accurate decoding?
    A.   Decoding relies on advanced oral language skills and expressive vocabulary.
    B.   Decoding includes making meaning of a word after it has been sounded out.
    C.   ELLs may struggle with digraphs not present in their native language.
    D.   ELLs may struggle with orthographic conventions.

14) Mr. Ramirez's co-teacher has asked that he help introduce the following new vocabulary to his third-grade class to help prepare students for an upcoming math lesson:

parallel, congruent, rhombus, trapezoid

Which of the following concepts is being developed in the students?
    A.   content-specific words
    B.   multiple-meaning words
    C.   different registers
    D.   figurative language

15) To help students expand their vocabulary based on root words they already know, they can be instructed in:
    A.   common derivational morphemes
    B.   etymologies
    C.   creating and using word walls
    D.   syllabication

16) In a conference with the parents of a second grade student, a teacher wants to provide suggestions for practice at home to improve fluency. Which strategy should the teacher suggest?

A. timed silent reading
B. cloze exercises
C. reading aloud to a younger sibling
D. listening to an older sibling read aloud

17) A fifth grade teacher is helping students understand subtle shades of meaning and connotations of words. Which vocabulary-building activity is most appropriate?
A. semantic gradients
B. possible sentences
C. morphological analysis
D. word wall

18) A second grade teacher wants to assess fluency during silent reading. Which strategy would best meet this goal?
A. observation as students turn the pages of a book
B. a timed passage-based comprehension assessment
C. students write a journal entry in response to a text
D. an exit ticket at the end of class

19) According to Scarborough's strands of the reading rope, what is most likely to make reading become more automatic?
A. background knowledge
B. vocabulary knowledge
C. word recognition
D. understanding of language structure

20) Which text type would be most appropriate for use to assess oral fluency?
A. a familiar text at the independent or instructional reading level
B. an unfamiliar text at the instructional or frustration level
C. any unfamiliar text
D. any literary text

21) A third-grade ELL student is struggling to meet the teacher's goals for proficient prosody during oral reading assessments. What is the best course of action for the teacher to take?
A. have the student read the same text multiple times
B. ask the student to slow down the reading rate
C. encourage the student to use graphophonic cueing
D. give the student texts with rhyme or dialogue

Constructed Response

1) At the beginning of the year, a first-grade teacher does a screener to assess students' current literacy development. One student's responses are presented below:

Question	Student Response
Can you say a word that rhymes with cat?	Coke.
Can you say a word that rhymes with hide?	Hand.
Now I'll say some word parts. Tell me how many sounds you hear in the word. d-og gr-ape	one one
Now I'll say some words. You say a word that has the same beginning sound. Red Ride Run Rip Can you say a word that has the same beginning sound?	Roll.

- Describe ONE aspect of the student's current literacy development that requires further development and evidence from the assessment to back up this assertion.

- Describe TWO strategies to help the student develop this aspect of emergent literacy.

2) A second-grade teacher provides small group interventions as part of a multi-tiered system of support. During a session, a student reads the following text:

Text	Student's Reading
I like driving with my mom. She drives faster than my dad. My dad hates speed.	I luck driiv-ing with mom. She drivs fast than dad. My dad hats spid.

- Identify TWO specific challenges this student is having with accurate and fluent decoding and specific evidence from the student's reading to back up each assertion.

- Recommend ONE strategy to help the student overcome EACH of these challenges.

3) A fifth-grade student diagnosed with dyslexia is struggling to comprehend her content-area textbooks. Prior to the next IEP meeting, her reading teacher and special education teacher are brainstorming ideas to help the student better access textbook content.

- List TWO recommendations that the team could make to help this student.

- Describe how EACH strategy is likely to benefit the student.

Answer Key 2

Phonological and Phonemic Awareness/Emergent Literacy

1) **C.** He did not sound out the word into onset *fl* and rime *at*.

2) **B.** His students will delete a sound from each word to make a new word.

3) **A.** As students listen to stories being read, they learn new words and learn about the syntactic structure of oral language.

4) **B.** Students are connecting onsets and rimes to make words.

5) **C.** Students can use a letter-sound chart to check off each phoneme, or letter sound, they know.

6) **B.** Signs and labels in the classroom are good sources of environmental print that can help students develop print awareness.

7) **C.** This question would help students identify the conflict and is age appropriate.

8) **C.** This activity helps students in both comprehension of the story and understanding its organization in having a beginning, middle, and end.

9) **C.** The teacher said the individual letter sounds and asked Johnny to blend them into a word.

10) **B.** This activity will help Mr. Hawks identify which students know which words and what words they need to practice more.

11) **B.** There are forty-four distinct phonemes, or units of sound, in the English language.

12) **B.** Encoding or translating sounds into letters will also be a problem with a student who is struggling to decode because the two processes are related.

13) **B.** To determine how to best help this student, the teacher should assess whether or not he has mastered the letter sounds, as that is knowledge needed to sound out CVC words.

14) **D.** This question allows students to make a predication, which goes beyond simple recall or literal comprehension as in the other questions.

Phonics and Decoding

1) **C.** An individual assessment is the best way to determine individual student knowledge.

2) **C.** Graphemes are ways of recording a sound. So the teacher could explain that sometimes the same sound has a different grapheme.

3) **A.** Phonemic awareness is an understanding of how phonemes can be orally manipulated to change the meanings of words.

4) **C.** R-controlled vowels are vowels followed by the letter r.

5) **C.** Part of metacognition is assessing one's own understanding; this would be the first step before applying fix-up strategies.

6) **A.** This word has two consonants, a vowel, and then a final end consonant.

7) **B.** Vocabulary instruction and automatic word recognition are effective strategies for ELLs.

8) **D.** Dipthongs are vowel sounds that change from the standard a, e, i, o, u sounds. In this word, -ough makes an -ew sound.

9) **D.** Explicit phonics instruction is teacher- guided and focuses on decoding strategies rooted in phonics.

10) **B.** This will help these students know that these are long vowel sounds. The other options are too advanced for students who are not yet automatic word readers.

11) **B.** Multisensory approaches use multiple senses. In this case, students are saying the words as they are using a tactile approach by writing in the sand.

12) **C.** Specific word-reading difficulty refers to students who have trouble reading or decoding individual words.

13) **B.** This shows a steady increase from least to most difficult.

14) **D.** Elkonin boxes present words divided into phonemes or syllables, so this would be the best tool.

15) **C.** A reader who does not pause at commas or stop at periods or use inflection for questions will not read with prosody or appropriate expression.

16) **A.** Recursive phonics instruction involves repetition of the same sounds, patterns, and skills. This is how students master them.

Comprehension of Literary and Informational Text

1) **D.** Having students write down what they know about the topic will help them retrieve background information about space exploration to set them up for more successful comprehension of the passage.

2) **C.** Setting a purpose helps students think about the purpose they will have for reading different types of texts.

3) **D.** Slowing the reading rate is a helpful fix-up strategy when comprehension breaks down, and it can increase comprehension of challenging parts of a text.

4) **B.** 770L is an appropriate text measure for a fourth-grade student's level of proficiency.

5) **C.** The character map can help readers organize thoughts on how the girl looks, acts, feels, and speaks.

6) **D.** Students may not be familiar with the historical era in which the novel is set, and having this information about setting can help them better comprehend the novel.

7) **D.** The central idea is the particular point the author is making about the topic.

8) **A.** A story with a linear, predictable plot is most appropriate for introducing this concept.

9) **C.** Comparing a fiction and nonfiction text on the same topic can help students understand how the genres differ.

10) **B.** Texts at the instructional level should be used for teacher-guided instruction.

11) **C.** Students are making text-to-text connections by comparing and contrasting two different texts on the same topic.

12) **A.** An Informal Reading Inventory (IRI) helps determine a student's independent, frustrational, and instructional reading levels, making it a useful tool for grouping.

13) **C.** Universal screening, or screening of all students, allows for early and prompt interventions for students who might have reading difficulties.

14) **B.** Before students read, they should predict what the text will be about based on the title, bolded words, heading, pictures, etc.

15) **C.** Students set their own goals and track their progress which encourages self-directed learning.

16) **C.** It is possible that students may need help deciphering dialogue written in a different dialect or regional speech pattern.

17) **A.** The point of view, or the viewpoint from which a story is told, is a structural element of literature.

18) **B.** She is helping her students guess what they think might happen.

19) **B.** This is a great introductory exercise to get students thinking about summaries.

20) **C.** This is the characteristic of many narratives written in the first-person point of view.

21) **C.** The teacher is helping students become attuned to the differences in multiple sources of information such as sources that include visuals and those that do not and sources that have large print and those that have smaller print.

22) **A.** Literal comprehension is the most basic level of comprehension, so asking where a story takes place is the best question to assess this skill.

Writing Skills and Processes

1) **B.** Copying is a key stage in learning to write, and a child's name is a word with which she is generally already familiar.

2) **B.** Research suggests that the study of grammar through isolated drill is ineffective. No evidence supports the other assertions.

3) **C.** Considering audience will help the student think about how to best communicate his message clearly to the reader.

4) **A.** Using homophones correctly allows students to apply what they have learned and see the connection to their own writing.

5) **C.** In shared writing, the teacher scribes for the students, making it a beneficial activity for students with physical disabilities that impact fine motor skills.

6) **B.** Words at the instructional spelling level can be spelled with 40 – 90 percent accuracy.

7) **A.** Combining instruction in pronouns with point of view is a logical way to integrate these two concepts; they are extensions of each other.

8) **D.** This is a common spelling convention, or orthographic pattern, present in English.

9) **C.** Publishing is the last stage in the writing process.

10) **D.** This student is helping her peer ensure his writing remains true to its overall point or focus.

11) **C.** Word sorts are a way for students to sort spelling words into categories based on orthographic patterns.

12) **D.** Using framed paragraphs, students fill in scripted blanks in a paragraph with a focus on organization and coherence.

13) **B.** The student's writing is mostly run-on sentences and fragments, indicating that he needs explicit instruction in sentence structure.

14) **A.** Peer review activities should occur within a carefully structured framework so that students have explicit and targeted tasks.

15) **B.** Informal language could communicate a message just as effectively in a poem written without a set structure.

16) **A.** Successful mechanics instruction encourages students to see that mechanics help communicate meaning to the reader.

Vocabulary and Fluency

1) **C.** In reader's theater, students read aloud different parts, focusing on reading with expression.

2) **C.** Texts should be familiar to students, as this will help them develop fluency.

3) **A.** Heterogenous grouping allows more proficient oral readers to model for peers.

4) **A.** Rate is the speed at which one reads.

5) **C.** Sight word instruction is designed to help students recognize high-frequency words automatically, without decoding, so they can read with fluency.

6) **D.** This would likely help the student to better keep track of the specific part of the text being read.

7) **A.** Derivational morphemes are affixes that are added to root words. This would help students build on vocabulary knowledge they already have by learning new forms of a word.

8) **C.** This may help the student's confidence if he is familiar with the text.

9) **B.** The teacher is giving students options of how they can complete the assignment, which is a key part of the Universal Design for Learning (UDL).

10) **C.** These affixes all change a base word into a different part of speech, so this could be easily integrated.

11) **B.** This student is likely quite advanced and may benefit from enrichment opportunities.

12) **C.** Explicit vocabulary instruction, such as lessons on common idioms, will aid ELLs the most.

13) **B.** To truly decode, a student must know the meaning of the word after sounding it out. ELLs may need exposure to basic English vocabulary to help in this process.

14) **A.** The students need a basic knowledge of the meaning of these words before they can apply them in math class.

15) **A.** Derivational morphemes are affixes that are added to root words. This would help students build on vocabulary knowledge they already have by learning new forms of a word.

16) **C.** This is most likely to improve fluency and be achievable in a home environment.

17) **A.** Semantic gradients are scales or lines that show two extreme opposite words. Students then add other words with similar meanings along the scale or line.

18) **B.** The time element will assess rate and automaticity. The comprehension element will also assess whether students actually read the passage efficiently (and for meaning) during the time allotted.

19) **C.** Word recognition skills such as phonological awareness, decoding, and sight recognition is the second strand of the reading rope that leads to increasingly automatic reading. The other options fall under language comprehension, which makes reading increasingly strategic.

20) **A.** Familiar texts near the student's reading level are best for fluency assessment as other texts are likely to be too challenging.

21) **A.** This is most likely to help this student because of the nuances of English pronunciation.

Constructed Response

1) SAMPLE ANSWER

The student is struggling with basic phonological awareness or the ability to recognize sounds in words. This is evidenced by the student's inability to rhyme words with "cat" and "hide." It is further evidenced by the student's inability to recognize the onset-rime in "d-og" and "gr-ape." Though the teacher reads the words in two parts, the student only "hears" one sound.

To help build the student's phonological awareness, the student could benefit from activities to identify onset and rime such as Elkonin boxes where the student would say the onset and rime and move a magnet or tile as he or she says each word part. Another instructional strategy would be to help the student recognize rhyming words by using word families. For example, the student could use cards with a rhyming ending like "-og" and then move cards with an initial sound to each to make rhymes like "h-og," "f-og," and "l-og."

2) SAMPLE ANSWER

The student is struggling with long vowel sounds. This is evidenced by the student saying a short /i/ instead of a long /i/ in both "driving" and "drives" and a short /a/ in "hates" as well as a short /i/instead of a long /e/ for speed. The student has also omitted some words and word parts while reading such as "my" and the "er" in "faster."

To help the student master long vowel sounds, one recommendation is to have the student practice identifying and reading words with a vowel-consonant-silent e. This would help the student read "drives" and "hates," which follow this pattern. Another technique to help the student would be use of finger-tracking or pencil-tracking to help the student ensure that each word is read. In this method, the student would move the finger or pencil under each sound or each word to ensure that each word or word part is read and not skipped over.

3) SAMPLE ANSWER

The first recommendation is to provide copies of these textbooks in audio format. The second recommendation is to use line readers or reading strips. Both options are likely to benefit the student.

Students with dyslexia may struggle with the volume of text in a chapter of a fifth-grade content-area text and may feel overwhelmed. As they are struggling to decode this much text, they may miss

important content. An audio version of the book can support students reading the chapter. As the audio book plays (and it can often be adjusted to a slower rate), the student can follow along in the textbook. This still allows the student to read the textbook and will help improve comprehension. Students with dyslexia may also struggle with focusing on just the particular sentence or line of text they are reading. A line reader puts the specific sentence in question in focus for the student so that they can block out the text before and after it. Such a device is easy to use and can help students with dyslexia keep their place while reading content-area textbooks that may have lots of sentences on each page.

ONLINE RESOURCES

T rivium includes online resources with the purchase of this study guide to help you fully prepare for the exam.

From Stress to Success

Watch "From Stress to Success," a brief but insightful YouTube video that offers the tips, tricks, and secrets experts use to score higher on the exam.

Flashcards

Trivium's flash cards allow you to review important terms easily on your computer or smartphone.

Cheat Sheets

Review the core skills you need to master the exam with easy-to-read Cheat Sheets.

Feedback

Leave a review, send us helpful feedback, or sign up for Cirrus promotions—including free books!

Access these materials at: www.cirrustestprep.com/praxis-reading-5205-online-resources

Made in United States
Troutdale, OR
03/08/2024

18314409R00093